T0286761

BRITAIN'S MOTORWAYS

MARK CHATTERTON

AMBERLEY

This book is dedicated to all the groups and their road crews who have travelled the length of Britain's motorways to and from gigs.

Also by the Author

British Motorways: An Introduction
British Road Bridges: An Introduction
British Road Tunnels: An Introduction
Britain's Road Tunnels

First published 2022

Amberley Publishing
The Hill, Stroud,
Gloucestershire, GL5 4EP

www.amberley-books.com

Copyright © Mark Chatterton, 2022

The right of Mark Chatterton to be identified as the Author
of this work has been asserted in accordance with the
Copyright, Designs and Patents Act 1988.

ISBN: 978 1 3981 1116 5 (print)
ISBN: 978 1 3981 1117 2 (ebook)

British Library Cataloguing in Publication Data.
A catalogue record for this book is available from the British Library.

Typeset in 10pt on 13pt Celeste.
Typesetting by SJmagic DESIGN SERVICES, India.
Printed in the UK.

Contents

Introduction

Motorways have been in existence in Britain for over sixty years and have become part of our everyday lives. Yet we tend to have a love-hate relationship with them. We like them when everything is running smoothly and there are no traffic jams to hold us up, but when we can't get from A to B as we hoped, then we hate them. Millions of us use motorways every day, yet we tend to take them for granted. Motorways have helped transform the British economy and open up the country; they help us to visit people and places much quicker than before and initially they helped to get rid of traffic jams from many towns and cities.

Every day on the radio or television we are used to hearing news bulletins where there is a hold up somewhere on a motorway. As a result, we are now familiar with far-flung places like Chertsey or Holmes Chapel. Motorways have even got into our everyday language, with such words and phrases as 'motorway madness', 'contraflow' or 'rubbernecking'. There are also plenty of songs about motorways, such as Tom Robinson's *2,4,6,8 – Motorway* and Chris Rea's *The Road Hell*.

Yet the story of how Britain got its motorways is one of both success and failure. It includes political wranglings, U-turns and inactivity; environmental protests and public enquiries; not forgetting forced evictions through compulsory purchase leading to many people losing their homes, their land, their farms and their businesses to make way for a motorway. Then there are the motorways themselves. What many people don't realise is that there are plenty of unfinished motorways out there; not to mention missing junctions, secret junctions, non-stop roadworks and motorway closures for all sorts of reasons, some of which will be discussed in the pages of this book.

When it came to building motorways, Britain was much slower getting off the mark than our cousins in Europe and across the Atlantic, who had built thousands of miles of motorways by the time the post-war Special Roads Act for motorways was passed in 1949. It would be almost ten years before Britain got its first motorway – the Preston Bypass – even if it was only 8 miles long. Wait another year and the M1 had been opened, showing that we meant business. Hyped as the London to Birmingham motorway, in reality it started in Watford in Hertfordshire and only went as far as Rugby – 30 miles short of Birmingham.

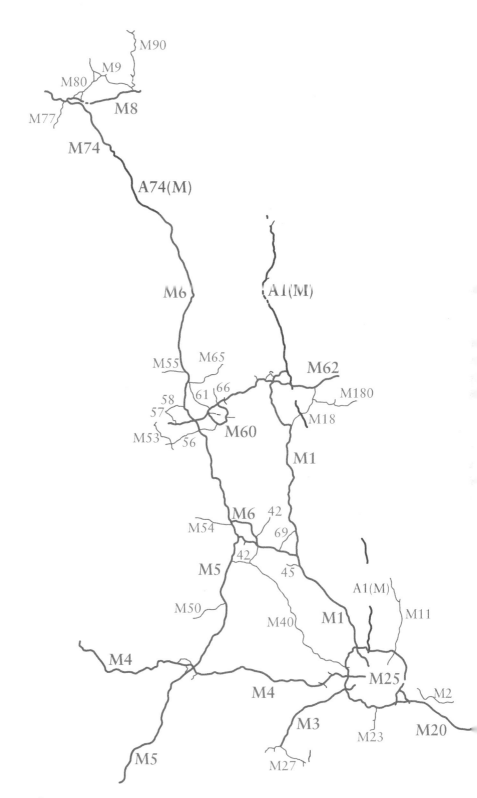

The main motorways of Britain.

Yet the 1960s and 1970s could be said to be the golden age of motorway building, with most of the M1, M2, M3, M4, M5, M6, M8, M9 and other motorways all built. The 1980s saw no let up, with the M25 opening in 1986; yet, by the 1990s motorway construction had slowed down considerably.

Now over twenty years into the twenty-first century, a new motorway being built seems like a dream to most people. There are just a handful of motorways that have been built or added to since the year 2000, and most of these are in Scotland. The last full-length motorway to be built in England was the M6 Toll, which opened in 2003 and was paid for by private investment. Perhaps that might be the way more motorways will be built in the future. Certainly, cost is one thing that has put governments off from building more motorways. The environmental argument is another factor, with climate change and the emphasis on becoming carbon neutral by 2050. Instead, the current picture seems to be on widening existing motorways to cater for increased demand. Yet, the conversion of hard shoulders to 'all lane running' is not popular with a lot of motorists, not least because of the potential danger a breakdown in a live lane can have. The idea of 'smart motorways' is one that has been promoted to the motorist in the past ten years, yet whether more of these will be built or not is a controversial topic.

In this book I have discussed every motorway that exists in Britain today, as well as those former motorways that have been downgraded to A roads. I look at the history of each motorway, such as when it was built, why it was built, how long it is and I mention any special features about it. I have also provided photographs of every current motorway, plus photos of things that you see as part of your motorway journey, and what they are there for.

I have personally travelled on every motorway there is in Great Britain, both as a driver and as a passenger, and learnt a great deal about them during the writing of this book. To the best of my knowledge all the information that I have provided in this book is correct at the time of writing, though things can change, such as a motorway being downgraded or its status being changed to a 'smart motorway'. So, sit back and enjoy the ride as you travel around Britain and along its many motorways.

1
Common Features of Motorways

Britain's motorways have certain features that help to make up the motorways we have today. Here are the most important:

The signage on motorways has been this distinct blue from the late 1950s when it was chosen by designers Jock Kinneir and Margaret Calvert. They also designed the fonts – called 'Transport' for the lower-case lettering and 'Motorway' for the route numbers. Blue is also used on maps to designate a motorway. The signs here show the routes for three different motorways – the M60, M62 and M66.

The central reservation is a gap between the two lanes of carriageway that may have grass or even hedges growing on it. There are usually crash barriers on both sides to prevent traffic crossing onto the opposing carriageway in the event of an accident. The crash barrier can either be in the form of steel or concrete, as in this example on the M25. (Wendy Chatterton)

Left: Driver location signs are the blue square signs showing the number of the motorway, either a letter A or B (indicating which direction you are travelling in) and some numbers showing how far from the start of the motorway you are in kilometres. This example is from the M56, going westbound, and is 59 km from the start of the motorway.

Below: Hard shoulders are areas of road to the left of the motorway carriageway, used by vehicles that break down or so those who need to stop in an emergency can do so. It can also be used by emergency vehicles when the motorway is blocked. This example is from the M53. (Howard Johnston)

Above: Overhead gantries are used to house electronic signs that can light up with a certain speed limit or show that a certain lane is closed in order to keep the traffic flowing. They also contain speed cameras to deter motorists from breaking the speed limit and cameras that record the number of vehicles using the motorway. The example here, from the A38 (M) in Birmingham, shows a 40 mph speed limit and three lanes that are closed to southbound traffic.

Below: Secret junctions are junctions or exits on motorways that are not allowed to be used by the ordinary motorist. Usually, they are marked by a blue 'Works unit only' sign. Most of them are for use by emergency vehicles to enter or exit the motorway when the road is blocked, or by motorway workers for entry to a maintenance depot. In some case they are used by the military to enter a nearby establishment. The one pictured here is on the eastbound carriageway of the M4 between junctions and 13 and 14. (Wendy Chatterton)

Above: Smart motorways have developed over time from traffic management systems, whereby the speed of the traffic was controlled from a control centre in order to stop queues due to heavy traffic. Now they are used to implement 'all lane running' when there is a need for the hard shoulder to be used for traffic when numbers demand. The one here is on the M42 near Solihull and shows a refuge area in yellow that can be used instead of the hard shoulder if a vehicle breaks down.

Below: From the earliest days of motorways telephones were placed 1 mile apart on each carriageway, so that if a motorist broke down they could walk to the nearest telephone and call for help. The one pictured is by the side of the M1 in Hendon.

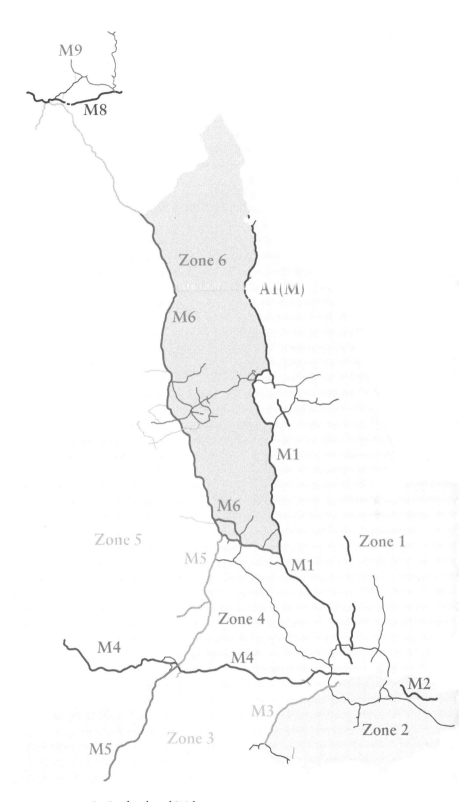

The different motorway zones in England and Wales.

2

M-designated Motorways

M1

The M1 was Britain's first purpose-built, long-distance motorway and is the second oldest motorway in Britain, being opened on 2 November 1959 by Ernest Marples, the Minister of Transport at the time. It followed the Preston Bypass, which had opened on 5 December 1958 and later became part of the M6. There had been plans to build a motorway between London and Birmingham as early as the 1920s, but it wasn't until the 1950s that it finally got the green light from the government.

It initially ran from the A41 near Watford, Hertfordshire (now junction 5), to the A5 near Rugby, Warwickshire, at what is now junction 18. It had two spur motorways at either end: the M10 going from junction 7 towards St Albans and the A5/A6 at its southern end, and the M45 going from junction 17 towards Coventry and Birmingham via the A45 at its northern end. The reason for this was to redistribute some of the traffic away from each end of the M1 so that they didn't get clogged up.

Back then, the M1 was about 60 miles in length and was seen as an 'intercity motorway' between London and Birmingham, even if it didn't quite reach these two cities. It was heralded as a revolution in road transport, as the motorway did not allow vehicles to stop on it, it had no speed limit, it had three lanes for most of its route and any roads crossing its route did so on bridges or roundabouts over or under the motorway. Many of these architectural features were designed by Owen Williams, and some of these are still in place today.

With the opening of the M1, it was possible to go non-stop all the way along the motorway, which led to many motorists and motor cyclists aiming to reach the speed of 100 mph as a badge of honour. In fact, the rally driver Jack Sears claimed to have reached a top speed of 185 mph on the M1 in June 1964. By December 1965, the 70-mph speed limit that we have on motorways came into force, initially as a trial, and then as law the following year.

The M1 north of Rugby was built in various stages between 1965 and 1968, when it became continuous all the way to junction 44 on the southern edge of Leeds, with the motorway being promoted as the 'London to Yorkshire motorway'. A final section into the centre of Leeds was opened in 1972, known as the Leeds South Eastern Motorway.

The start of the M1 at Staples Corner in Hendon, North London. This is one of two entrances to the motorway, with the other one starting at the other side of the roundabout and joining this carriageway on a flyover on the right.

This section north of junction 43 was renamed the M621 in 1999, as the M1 was extended further east to join with the A1 (M) at Hook Moor (junction 48), the final junction on the M1, giving it a total length of 193.5 miles (311.4 km).

Originally the M1 was planned to split into two routes in South Yorkshire at junction 32, with the main route going to Doncaster and the A1, while the other went towards Sheffield and Leeds. In the end the route to Doncaster became the M18 while the western route to Leeds became the primary route for the M1. At the southern end of the M1 the motorway was extended further south from junction 5 in different stages between the years 1966 and 1977, with junctions 1 to 2 being the last to be completed in July 1977. This is where the M1 meets the A604, the North Circular Road, though there were plans to take the M1 further south into London on a flyover as far as West Hampstead. Here the M1 would join up with the 'London Motorway Box', part of the ill-fated Ringway Project of concentric motorways going all around London from different points.

The M1 originally didn't have any lighting, crash barriers or hard shoulders (instead it had 'soft shoulders'), but these all were added later. The first crash barriers to be built on the M1 were between junction 24 (Kegworth) and junction 30 (Barlborough) in 1973. Lights were first introduced in the years 1972–73 between junctions 3 and 14, and junctions 16 to 24, while hard shoulders were built from the early 1960s onwards. The motorway has

The M1 under construction in 1959. This view is looking northwards at Chalton, near Toddington services. (Photo courtesy of Ben Brooksbank, cc-by-sa/2.0)

also been widened from two to three and then to four lanes in many places, and several of the motorway's junctions have been updated, so traffic flow and safety is improved, including the ones at Catthorpe where the M6 and A14 meet the M1, and Lofthouse where the M1 and M62 cross. Several new junctions have also been added to the M1, including junctions 6A, 21A, 23A, 24A, 29A and 35A. The motorway has also been changed into a smart motorway between junctions 10 and 13, with the hard shoulders turned into live running lanes. Other sections, including junctions 6A–10 and 25–28, have been widened to four lanes and variable speed limits added.

One new feature of motorway journeys was the introduction of the motorway service station, where motorists could get petrol, have a toilet break or have a meal. The first ones to be fully opened were on the M1 at Newport Pagnell on 15 August 1960, followed by the one at Watford Gap a month later. Early service stations featured a viewing walkway over the carriageway and upmarket restaurants. The most southerly one on the M1, the London Gateway services (formerly known as Scratchwood Services), uses the missing junction 3 as its access road and was opened in 1969.

Over the years there have been several significant events that have caused the motorway to be closed in parts. The most memorable event happened on 6 September 1997 when the funeral of Princess Diana took place, with the funeral hearse travelling north on the M1 between junctions 1 and 15A. Film taken on the day shows thousands of people standing on each bridge over the route, with thousands more standing by the side of the motorway, or in parts actually on the northbound carriageway. Near junction 9, some motorists actually parked their cars in the third lane of the southbound carriageway, got out and stood by the safety barrier to watch the hearse go past, despite the fact that traffic was still moving on this side of the motorway!

Another event that closed the M1 was in December 2005 when the explosion and fire at the Buncefield Oil depot, near to junction 8, occurred. As a result, the motorway was closed between junctions 6a and 12. Then, in April 2011, a fire at a scrapyard by an elevated section of the motorway in North London caused the M1 to be closed between junctions 1 and 4 from 15 to 21 April.

The M1 has been used as a location for feature films, including *Charlie Bubbles* (1968), *Birthday Girl* (2001) *28 Days Later* (2002), *Layer Cake* (2004) and *Hush* (2008). The motorway passes near the following major towns and cities: Watford, St Albans, Hemel Hempstead, Luton, Milton Keynes, Northampton, Rugby, Leicester, Loughborough, Derby, Nottingham, Mansfield, Chesterfield, Sheffield, Rotherham, Barnsley, Wakefield and Leeds. It has connections with the following motorways: M6, M18, M25, M45, M62, M69, M621 and the A1 (M). It is also part of European Route E13.

Looking south on the M1 shortly before it ends to meet the North Circular Road in London.

M2

The M2 is a 26-mile-long (42 km) motorway that is solely in Kent. It starts at Strood, near Rochester, where the A2 becomes the M2, and crosses over the River Medway on the Medway Viaduct, before ending on the eastern side of Faversham. Here the road splits into the A2, going south to Dover, and the A299, going east to Margate. It is the only M-designated motorway not joined to the national network of motorways, being separated from the M25 by just 10 miles. It is also unusual in that it has a mixture of two-, three- and four-lane carriageways along its route. It was built in sections in the 1960s, initially as a bypass for the Medway towns of Rochester, Chatham and Gillingham.

The first section to be opened was on 29 May 1963 between junctions 2 to 5 by Ernest Marples, the Transport Minister at the time. This was followed two years later by the other two sections: junctions 1 to 2 in the west, and junctions 5 to 7 in the east. It was initially going to be called the 'A2(M)', but after it was called the 'M2' in *The Daily Telegraph*, the designation M2 was used by the Ministry of Transport. It was envisaged that London

The start of the M2 at Strood, Kent, looking eastwards. (Wendy Chatterton)

would be linked with Dover by a continuous motorway, but this never happened. Instead, the M20 became the main motorway link between these two places.

Over the years the motorway and its junctions have been improved somewhat. In the years 2000 to 2003 the M2 was widened from two to four lanes between junctions 1 and 4, including a second Medway Viaduct being built. There is just once set of services on the motorway between junctions 4 and 5, known today as Medway services. They had originally been called Farthing Corner services.

One notable thing that happened on the M2 occurred in February 2014 when a large hole appeared on the motorway near Lynstead, which caused the motorway to be closed between junctions 5 and 6 for several days. It was found to be a dene hole, or chalk well, which was actually in the central reservation and is said to have been caused by heavy rain washing away earth that had been used to fill it in when the motorway was first constructed.

The M2 passes near the following towns: Rochester, Chatham, Gillingham, Rainham, Sittingbourne and Faversham. Part of its route runs parallel with the High Speed 1 railway line.

The M2 looking eastwards as it goes over the River Medway in Kent on the Medway Bridge. Note the HS1 railway line on the right. (Wendy Chatterton)

M3

The M3 is a motorway that connects London and parts of the South East with Southampton, the south coast and the West Country. It runs in a south-westerly direction from Sunbury-on-Thames on the edge of Greater London within the M25 to the outskirts of Southampton, where it meets up with M27. It is 59 miles (95 km) in length and was originally opened in June 1971 when the section from Lightwater (junction 3) to Popham, near Basingstoke (junction 8), was completed at a cost of £46 million.

Other sections were opened between the years 1974 and 1991, with the missing link to the south of Winchester between junctions 10 and 12 eventually opened in June 1995 after a series of public enquiries and many protests. This was because the missing section would go through St Catherine's Hill on Twyford Down in Hampshire, an ancient hill fort of great historical significance, and an Area of Special Scientific Interest. Rather than routing the motorway via a tunnel, it went through a deep cutting on part of the hill, which involved the destruction of an area of natural beauty and scientific significance. The protests, which began here, have led to a heightened awareness of the loss of countryside to motorways (and new roads in general), which in turn has affected future motorway building in Britain.

One amusing thing that happened on the motorway was that on 1 April 2000 a zebra crossing was painted across the northbound carriageway by pranksters between junctions 4 and 4A. It was quickly removed by maintenance staff. There are just two services on the M3. These are at Fleet and Winchester, which opened in 1973 and 2001 respectively. The M3 passes near the following towns and cities: Camberley, Farnborough, Basingstoke, Winchester, Eastleigh and Southampton. It connects with the M25 and M27. It is also part of European Route E05.

The start of the M3 from the A316, looking westwards at Sunbury-on-Thames, Surrey.

M4

The M4 is a 189-mile-long (304 km) motorway that runs from Chiswick in West London to Pont Abraham, Carmarthenshire, in South Wales, where it joins up with the A48. It was originally known as the 'London–South Wales motorway' and was built as an alternative route to the A4 in England and the A48 in Wales, as well as the A40, which ran through Gloucester, where the lowest crossing point of the River Severn between England and Wales was. It is also used by traffic from London and the South East going to Cornwall and Devon as an alternative route to the M3/A303.

The construction of the M4 was built piecemeal over a period of more than thirty years from 1959 to 1994. The first section of the M4 to be built was the Chiswick Flyover, which opened in September 1959. This was part of the A4 until March 1965 when the section of the M4 containing junctions 1 to 5 was opened. Similarly, the section known as the Maidenhead Bypass (junctions 7 to 9) was originally opened in May 1961 as the A4 (M), but when the Slough to Maidenhead section (junctions 5 to 7) opened in March 1963 it was renumbered the M4. The rest of the motorway was opened in different parts of England and Wales between March 1965 and June 1996 when the Second Severn Crossing was opened.

The original Severn Bridge between Aust and Mathern, carrying the M4 over the River Severn, was opened by the Queen on 8 September 1966. For almost thirty years this was the route of the M4 between England and Wales, but ever-increasing traffic led to a second crossing over the River Severn being built, as well as new approach roads, and this was

The M4 has several spurs off it. The most well known is the Heathrow Spur, pictured here looking north to where it joins the M4 proper. (Wendy Chatterton)

fully opened in June 1996. As a result of the M4 now being rerouted further south from its original route, this section of motorway was renumbered the M48. At the same time the M49 was also opened connecting the bridge with the M5 on the English side of the river.

On the Welsh side of the bridge the M4 was originally scheduled to terminate just west of Newport at Tredegar Park, but it did eventually reach the outskirts of Cardiff in 1977, joining up with the A48 at St Mellons. When the motorway was extended beyond Cardiff in 1980 this short spur off the new route of the M4 north of Cardiff became the A48 (M). The final part of the M4 in Wales was completed in 1994 with the opening of the Britton Ferry motorway bridge by junction 42.

The M4 has several notable engineering features on its route. The Almondsbury interchange is where the M4 (junction 20) and M5 (junction 15) cross. This is a four-level stack interchange (or Maltese cross junction) where the main carriageways of the two motorways pass under the various link roads on four levels, with the traffic flowing freely in all four directions. In the summer and at rush hours the whole intersection can be clogged up with traffic, which is not helped by the nearby junction 16 of the M5, meaning that some traffic using it has to cut across lanes, causing extra delays. The whole intersection (junction 20) as well as the section from junction 19 has been a smart motorway since January 2014.

A few miles to the west of this is the Second Severn Crossing via the Prince of Wales Bridge, which was opened in 1996 by Prince Charles. It has three lanes, as opposed to two on the original Severn Bridge, and is designed to withstand high winds. The toll charges on both Severn bridges ended in December 2018.

One of the most impressive British motorway structures of all – the Second Severn Crossing (or, since 2018, the Prince of Wales Bridge), carrying the M4 between England and Wales.

Also in Wales is the Brynglas Tunnel in Newport, which opened in 1967. It was the first tunnel to be built on a British motorway. However, as the M4 changes from three to two lanes either side of the tunnels, there are often long tailbacks on either side. There were plans to construct a new motorway to the south of Newport to relieve congestion in the area, but these were dropped by the Welsh Assembly in 2019.

One controversial aspect of the M4 was the 3.5-mile-long bus lane, situated between Heathrow and the elevated section, which was on the lane next to the central reservation of the M4 going into London. This meant buses and other traffic allowed to use it had to cross lanes to get to it, while the rest of traffic using the motorway had to use two instead of the usual three lanes. It was in use between the years 1999 and 2010, and during the 2012 Olympics, but was closed once they had had finished.

Another thing that angered motorists using the M4 was the amount of speed cameras being used on sections of the motorway in Wiltshire. This led to a 'go-slow' on the M4 in April 2005 when two groups of motorists in convoys of several hundred cars drove on the motorway between Leigh Delamere and Membury services. They drove at around 55 mph for around 30 miles in total to make their protest. This was followed a few months later by a similar go-slow in South Wales, where drivers protesting about fuel prices drove along the M4 at 50 mph.

There are currently eleven motorway service areas on the M4, of which the one at Heston in West London is perhaps the most well known. It was seen as a location in the 2007 film *Hot Fuzz*. For many years there was sign before it that proclaimed, '106 miles to the next services'.

Finally, one of the biggest loads ever transported on Britain's roads travelled along the M4 westwards on a journey from Didcot Power Station in Oxfordshire to Avonmouth Docks in Avon in November 2013. It weighed 640 tonnes and travelled at just 4 mph, causing a 13-mile tailback.

The M4 passes near to the towns and cities of Slough, Maidenhead, Reading, Newbury, Swindon, Chippenham, Bristol, Newport, Cardiff, Bridgend, Port Talbot and Swansea. It connects to the following motorways: the M5, M25, M32, M48, M49, A48 (M), A308 (M), A329 (M) and A404 (M). It is also part of European Route E30.

The M4 in South Wales. Here the motorway crosses over the River Loughor, near Pontaddulais, not far from its terminus.

M5

The M5 runs from its junction with the M6 in West Bromwich in the West Midlands to Exeter in Devon for a distance of just under 163 miles (262.4 km). It was constructed to relieve the amount of traffic going between the West Midlands and the West Country and South Wales, mainly via the A38. The first section to be built was that between Lydiate Ash (junction 4) and the M50 (junction 8), which opened in July 1962 as a dual two-lane motorway. This later had to be widened to three lanes to cope with the amount of traffic using it. Another section bypassing Filton in Bristol (junctions 16–17) was also opened in 1962. The section from junction 4 to the M6 in Birmingham, including the Frankley services was built between 1967 and 1970, most of this being elevated motorway. The section south from the M50 through Gloucestershire and Somerset to Devon was built over a ten-year period between 1967 and 1977.

The Almondsbury Interchange to the north of Bristol where the M4 (junction 20) and the M5 (junction 15) meet was opened by the Queen on 8 September 1966. A few miles further south, the M5 crosses over the River Avon on the Avonmouth Bridge, which is 4,554 feet

The M5, looking north from junction 9 for Tewkesbury, on a summer's evening during rush hour.

(1,388 m) long. Work started on the bridge in 1969, but it was not until May 1974 that it was finally opened. One of the problems with it is its height, which was done to allow tall ships to sail underneath it, yet the steep gradients leading to its centre mean that lorries often slow down when crossing it, causing congestion. It has also been widened to four lanes each way and had its surface changed several times in its history, leading to many motorists believing that it has permanent roadworks on it. Nevertheless, its opening led to Bristol no longer being a major bottleneck for traffic going to and from the West Country.

South of the Avonmouth Bridge, between junctions 19 and 20, the M5 splits into two levels as the carriageway goes along the edge of Tickenham Hill, with impressive views over to the west. An interesting landmark next to the M5 to the south of junction 23 is the *Willow Man*, a 40-foot-high sculpture made out of willow withies that is sited by the northbound carriageway.

There are currently ten service areas on the M5, with Strensham services by the junction with the M50 being the oldest, having opened in November 1962. In 1991, when the junction here was remodelled, the northbound services were rebuilt about half a mile further to the north to help with the new traffic flow. The Midlands Air Ambulance use these services as an operational base.

The M5 passes either through or near to the cities and towns of Birmingham, Bromsgrove, Worcester, Cheltenham, Gloucester, Bristol, Weston-super-Mare, Bridgwater, Taunton and Exeter on its route. The M5 is connected to the following motorways: the M4, M6, M42, M49, M50.

The southbound Strensham services in 1964 – two years after opening. (Courtesy of Ben Brooksbank, cc-by-sa/2.0)

M6

The M6 is the longest motorway in Great Britain, with a length of 232.2 miles (373.7 km). It starts at Catthorpe, near Rugby in Warwickshire, where it leaves the M1 at junction 19 and goes via Birmingham and the north-west of England as far as the Scottish border at Gretna, near junction 45, where it continues as the A74 (M).

The first section of the M6 to be built was the 8-mile-long Preston Bypass (junctions 29 to 32), which was opened on 5 December 1958 by the prime minister at the time, Harold Macmillan. It was also the first section of motorway ever to be opened in Britain, though it wasn't renamed the M6 until it was joined to the section from junction 20, near Warrington, in July 1963.

The next section to be opened was the Lancaster Bypass (junctions 33 to 35) in April 1960, and for the next twelve years different parts of the M6 were opened at different locations up and down its route, with junctions 6 to 7 in Birmingham, which opened in May 1972, completing the M6 – or so most people thought. By then the motorway was continuous from the M1 all the way to junction 44, to the north of Carlisle. However, with the M74/A74 (M) motorway south from Glasgow reaching the Scottish–English border at Gretna in December 1992, there was a missing section of motorway between these two points nicknamed the 'Cumberland Gap'. This final section of the M6 was eventually opened in December 1998, being officially opened fifty years to the day after the first section of the M6 was opened on 5 December 1958. So, it might be argued that the M6 has the accolade of the longest time taken for a motorway to be constructed – in England, at least.

The start of the M6 at Catthorpe in Leicestershire, looking north from the M1. (Wendy Chatterton)

Being a long motorway, the M6 passes through a wide variety of landscapes in both urban and country areas. For the section through the northern part of Birmingham, it is very much an urban motorway, most of it being elevated above ground between junctions 5 and 9, including the Bromford Viaduct, which is the longest road viaduct in Britain. The well-known 'Spaghetti Junction', or Gravelly Hill Interchange, to give it its proper name, can be found at junction 6, where the M6 meets the A38 (M) coming up from Central Birmingham, as well as the A38 (Tyburn Road), the A5127 (Lichfield Road) and some more minor roads. It has five different levels and also crosses two rivers, three canals and two railway lines.

Further north near Warrington, the M6 crosses the River Mersey and the Manchester Ship Canal on the iconic Thelwall Viaduct. It is actually two separate bridges, the first of which opened in 1963, and the second opened in 1995. The section of the M6 between junctions 36 and 40 that passes through Cumbria is one of the most picturesque parts of the motorway network, especially when the motorway passes through the Lune Gorge. Where the M6 splits into two separate carriageways between junctions 38 and 39 there is an unusual sight in that a local road runs between the two carriageways. When the M6 goes over Shap Summit, which is 1,050 feet (320 m) above sea level, this is one the highest places for a motorway in Britain.

The motorway has had various improvements made to it over the years. These include the realignment of the Catthorpe Interchange in 2016, where the A14 meets the M1 and the M6 in a free-flowing junction. Plus, several parts of the M6 have been turned into a smart motorway, including between junctions 2–13 and 16–19.

The iconic tower at Lancaster services on the M6 in Lancashire. (Wendy Chatterton)

There are seventeen motorway service areas on the M6, with the one at Charnock Richard to the north of Wigan being the first to open in 1963, while the newest one at Rugby recently opened in 2021. The one at Lancaster services, between junctions 32 and 33, is notable for its futuristic-looking tower called the Pennine Tower. It was originally used as a restaurant and observation deck, but has been closed to the public since 1989. It is now Grade II listed.

The elevated section of the M6 near Walsall was used as a location for the 1970 film *Gimme Shelter*, starring the Rolling Stones. The public information film *Night Call* from 1977 was also filmed on the M6 around Birmingham, as was the 2013 psychological film drama *Locke*. The M6 is also said to be Britain's most haunted road, coming out on top of a survey to find Britain's most haunted roads. Sightings have included groups of Roman soldiers walking across the carriageway and a lorry driving the wrong way down the carriageway.

The M6 passes near to or through the towns and cities of Coventry, Birmingham, Walsall, Wolverhampton, Stafford, Stoke-on-Trent, Newcastle-under-Lyme, Crewe, Warrington, Wigan, Preston, Lancaster, Penrith and Carlisle. It intersects with these motorways: the M1, M5, M6 Toll, M42, M54, M55, M56, M58, M61, M62, M65, M69, A38 (M), A74 (M) and A 601 (M). It is part of the following European Routes: E05, E18, E22 and E24.

The famous RAC headquarters building next to the M6, near Walsall.

M6 Toll

The M6 Toll, also known as the 'Midland Expressway', is perhaps Britain's most controversial motorway, as it is the only motorway in Britain where a toll is made to motorists who travel along it. The motorway is 27 miles (43 km) long and runs across the north edge of Birmingham as an alternative to the M6 through Birmingham – hence its early name as the 'Birmingham Northern Relief Road'. It starts on the eastern edge of Birmingham and terminates to the south of Cannock. On its east side it runs concurrent with the M42 for 5 miles after it leaves the M6 proper at junction 3. It is rejoined to the M6 at junction 11A, near Wolverhampton in the north. It runs parallel with both the A5 and A38 trunk roads on part of its route.

It was first proposed as an alternative to the M6 via Birmingham in 1980, but it wasn't until 1989 that it finally got the go ahead with the condition that its cost would be privately funded. The company that won the contract was Midland Expressway Limited in 1991. Site clearance started in 2000 and it was finally opened in December 2003 – the only completely new motorway to open in England this century.

Apart from having to pay a toll to use it, motorists find that the way the M6 Toll is aligned means that the M6 lanes diverge from the main carriageway at either end, giving the impression that the M6 Toll is the main motorway. Those drivers who do not check the signs above the carriageway can easily find themselves on the toll motorway rather than the M6 and so have to pay the toll just to get off the motorway. Also, the name of the motorway, 'M6 Toll', is confusing for a lot of drivers as no other motorway in Britain has the same number as another motorway.

The start of the M6 Toll motorway near Wolverhampton, Staffordshire. Note the route of the M6 proper going off to the left. (Wendy Chatterton)

What is clear from almost twenty years of the M6 Toll is that it is one of Britain's least used motorways for its capacity, especially in regard to lorries and tankers who are put off using it by the high charge of the toll. In 2021, the toll charge was £7 for a car and £12.60 for a HGV lorry during peak hours, if you travelled the whole length of the motorway. However, those who do use it tend to be motorists on longer journeys up and down the country, who use it both for its quietness and for the time it saves compared to going on the M6 through Birmingham, which is often heavily congested.

One interesting fact about the motorway is that its surface is an amalgamation of pulped paperback novels. Another difference to other motorways is that the exits off the motorway to other roads are not numbered as with conventional motorway junctions but rather as numbers with the prefix 'T', e.g. T4. There were plans to join it with the M54 and to extend it further up the M6 as far as Knutsford, but both these plans were later dropped.

There is just one services on the motorway, known as Norton Carnes services. It came out as being in the top five motorway service stations in the country in a Which? consumer survey in 2021. On its route the motorway passes near to the towns and cities of Sutton Coalfield, Lichfield, Brownhills and Cannock. It is part of the European Route E05.

A quiet day for traffic using the M6 Toll motorway. (Wendy Chatterton)

M8

The M8 is Scotland's busiest and most important motorway, connecting Glasgow in the west with Edinburgh in the east. The motorway begins at junction 1 on the western fringes of Edinburgh, at its junction with the Edinburgh City Bypass, the A720, and goes in a westerly direction through the Central Belt towards Glasgow. It continues through the northern part of the city centre, before going south over the River Clyde on the Kingston Bridge and then going west again, past Glasgow Airport and ending at junction 31 at Bishopton in Renfrewshire, where it becomes the A8 towards Greenock.

For many years it was a motorway in two parts, with a 6-mile gap connected by the A8, between Baillieston and Newhouse (junctions 6 to 8), but in April 2017 this missing section was eventually opened, making the M8 60 miles (97 km) long. The first section to be opened was the Harthill Bypass by George Willis, the Minister of State for Scotland in 1965, while the section through Glasgow was constructed between 1968 and 1972. The other sections were added piecemeal until the motorway that exists today was finally completed in 2017, which is fifty-two years since the first section was opened.

The section through Glasgow suffers from frequent congestion, which is made worse because the M8 meets two other motorways, the M74 and the M77, south of the Kingston Bridge. The section through Glasgow is part of the now defunct Glasgow Inner Ring Road. It is unusual in that there are some exits on the right, as well as the closest exits on a

The M8, central Glasgow, crossing the River Clyde on the Kingston Bridge, looking west.

The M8 at Charing Cross, Glasgow, where it goes into a short tunnel.

motorway anywhere in Britain. This might be explained by the fact that the motorway was designed in a similar way to the American urban freeways. There is a short tunnel at Charing Cross in Glasgow and an elevated viaduct for several miles through Glasgow. There is just one services on the M8 at Harthill between junctions 4A and 5. It is called the Heart of Scotland services and opened in 1971.

The M8 passes through or near to the following towns and cities: Edinburgh, Livingston, Airdrie, Coatbridge, Glasgow, Paisley and Clydebank. It connects to the M9, M73, M74, M77, M80 and M898 motorways. It is part of the E05 and E16 European Routes.

M9

The M9 is a motorway in Scotland that begins at junction 2 of the M8 to the west of Edinburgh and ends at Dunblane (junction 11), where the A9 takes over. It was first opened in August 1968 when a section of the motorway (junctions 4 to 9) bypassed the towns of Polmont, Grangemouth, Falkirk and Stenhousemuir. The next section to be opened was the Newbridge Bypass in November 1970, between junctions 1 and 2. The remaining parts of the motorway, junctions 2 to 4 and 9 to 11, opened between the years 1971 and 1974.

The motorway is 33 miles (53.1 km) in length and is unusual for motorways in that it shares part of its route for 1 mile (1.6 km) with the M876, between junctions 7 and 8. The motorway is three lanes wide here, which is the furthest north in Britain for a three-lane motorway. To the south of Stirling, it is joined by the M80 coming north from Glasgow.

An interesting landmark that can be seen next to the motorway to the north of Falkirk are the *Kelpies*, two 30-metre-high horse sculptures made out of stainless steel and designed by sculptor Andy Scott. There is just one set of services on the motorway, Stirling services, which are accessed from junction 9 of the M9 and shared with the M80. Originally, there was a short spur of the M9 leading to the Forth Road Bridge, but with the opening of the newer Queensferry Crossing, this spur has now become part of the M90. The M9 connects with the M8, M80, M90 and M876.

Above: The M9 in Scotland, looking north-west, shortly before the section where it shares its route with the M876 for around a mile. (Wendy Chatterton)

Right: One of the most intriguing sites on Scotland's motorways are the Kelpies, two stainless-steel horse sculptures that are situated right next to the M9 near Falkirk. (Wendy Chatterton)

M11

The M11 starts in North East London on the A604, north circular road in two separate entrances and runs to the north-west of Cambridge, where it meets the A14 at junction 14. It actually starts at junction 4 rather than junction 1. The reason for this is that originally it would have started at Ringway 1, near Hackney, where an inner-ring motorway around London was envisaged. This road eventually became the A12 leading to the Blackwall Tunnel.

Plans for the M11 go back as far as 1915 when the idea of having an 'Eastern Avenue' in this part of North East London was first proposed. However, it wasn't until the 1960s that more definite plans were made with the route for a new motorway out of London to Stansted Airport, initially following the valley of the River Lea. However, the route was moved further east to follow the valley of the River Roding instead.

The first section of the M11 to be opened was that between junctions 7 and 8 (Harlow to Stansted) in 1975. The rest of the motorway was eventually completed in 1980, making it

The M11, looking south just before junction 8 for Bishop's Stortford. (Andrew Lamyman)

55 miles (88.5 km) in length. The section north of Stansted Airport has just two, as opposed to three, lanes. There have been calls for this part of the motorway to be widened to three lanes due to the problems of overtaking lorries causing tailbacks as they proceed up the steeper gradients in this section.

A major improvement to the motorway was the realignment of junction 8 where traffic for Stansted Airport met local traffic coming into and out of nearby Bishops Stortford. An

The M11, looking north between junctions 8A and 9, where it has just two lanes on each carriageway. This section is notorious for tailbacks when lorries struggle to overtake here due to the hilly terrain. (Wendy Chatterton)

extra junction, 8A, was opened in December 2002, which allowed airport traffic to flow freely from the motorway to the airport.

One notable incident in the history of the M11 took place overnight in January 2003 when several thousand motorists became stranded on the motorway between junctions 7 and 9 for almost twenty hours after some lorries jackknifed, in what became known as 'White Friday'. The M11 has just one services, Birchanger Green, just off junction 8. The motorway passes near to the towns and cities of Epping, Harlow, Bishops Stortford, Saffron Walden and Cambridge. It is connected to the M25.

M18

The M18 is a motorway in Yorkshire that runs from junction 32 of the M1 at Thurcroft in a north-easterly direction towards Goole, where it meets the M62 at junction 35. It is 26.5 miles (42.6 km) in length and joins up with the M180 at junction 5 where its only service area is, which is known as Doncaster North services. It helps traffic going from the M1 and A1(M) reach the Humber Estuary ports of Grimsby, Immingham and Hull, as well as East Yorkshire without the need of going over the Humber Bridge. The M18 also goes over the A1 (M) at junction 2, the Wadworth Viaduct, on a three-level stacked roundabout.

The M18 was originally going to be part of the route of the M1 going towards Doncaster. Instead, the M1 went on a route further west past Sheffield and up to Leeds and eventually the A1 (M). This explains why at junction 32 the M1 changes direction on an almost 90-degree angle, going in a westerly direction.

The first part of the M18 to be opened was the section between junction 1 to 2 in November 1967. The rest of the motorway was opened in stages between 1972 and 1977. The section between junctions 2 and 3 leading to Doncaster and Doncaster Sheffield Airport has been widened from two to three lanes to help with traffic flow. The M18 is connected to the M1, M62, M180 and A1 (M) and is part of Euroroutes E13 and E22.

The southbound carriageway of the M18 shortly before it joins the M1 in a triangular junction. (Wendy Chatterton)

M20

The M20 is situated in Kent and runs near the A20 for much of its route, starting at its junction with the M25 in the west to just beyond Folkestone in the east. The M20 is seen as the main route between London, the Channel Tunnel and the port of Dover, as opposed to the M2 further to the north. It has become synonymous as the parking area for HGVs waiting to cross the channel, known as 'Operation Stack'.

It is 51 miles (82 km) long and was originally opened in December 1960 between junctions 5 and 7 as the A20 (M) and called the Maidstone Bypass West. The following year, in September 1961, the Maidstone Bypass East was opened between junction 7 and 8 – again, as the A20 (M), though this was changed to the M20 in the 1970s. Over the next twenty years other parts of the M20 were opened in sections, so that by 1981 the M20 was complete apart from a 14-mile (23 km) gap between Maidstone and Ashford (junctions 8 to 9). It would not be until May 1991 that this missing link was finally opened due to the imminent opening of the Channel Tunnel, thirty years after the first part of the motorway had been opened.

In August 2016, part of a pedestrian footbridge over the motorway at Ryarsh was brought down, believed to have been hit by a low loader being moved along the hard shoulder. The whole bridge had to be demolished for safety reasons in September 2016 and it wasn't until March 2021 that a replacement foot and cycle bridge was opened. There are two service areas on the M20 at Maidstone (junction 8) and at Folkestone (junction 11). The M20 is routed near to the towns of Maidstone, Ashford and Folkestone. It is connected to the M25 and M26 and is part of Euroroute E15.

The M20 west of Maidstone in Kent, looking east, on a pleasant summer's day with, unusually, not a HGV in sight.

M23

The M23 runs from the A23 south of Hooley in Surrey to Pease Pottage in West Sussex, where it rejoins the A23 route south to Brighton, passing Gatwick Airport on its way. It starts at junction 7, as opposed to junction 1, just to the north of the M25. This is because it was originally going to start in London at Ringway 2, which was a proposed alternative route to the South Circular road. In the end junctions 1 to 6 of the proposed M23 were never built, partly due to opposition with much of the route going through London's suburbs and parkland, and partly through lack of government action.

The motorway is the main route from South London to Gatwick Airport, London's second airport, and as such has its own spur into the airport from junction 9. The M23 was opened between the years 1974 and 1975 – at the same time as part of the M25 (junctions 6 to 8). It is 15.9 miles (25.6 km) long and has just one service area by junction 11, known as Pease Pottage services. In 1997, a new junction, 10A, was opened to give access to the suburb of Crawley called Maidenbower. In 2020, the motorway between junctions 8 and 10 was converted into a smart motorway.

The southern end of the M23 looking north at Pease Pottage in West Sussex. The services are just behind the trees on the right.

M25

The M25 is Britain's most notorious motorway, mainly due to the number of traffic jams that occur on its 117-mile (188 km) length all around London. Known as the 'London Orbital Motorway', it is not in fact a complete circlular motorway, as the section of road known as the Dartford Crossing, where a bridge and two tunnels cross the River Thames, is actually the A282. Just to confuse things, junctions 1A and 1B are on the A282, while the first junction on the M25 is actually junction 2 (for the A2). At the other end of the M25 the final junction is junction 30 (for the A13), yet there is a junction 31 on the A282 (for the A1306), just a mile beyond the end of the M25.

The idea for a ring road around London first began in the 1930s. This had then evolved into the idea of having a series of ring roads, or 'ringways', in and around London by the 1960s. Work eventually began on this outer ringway in 1973, on the section between junctions 23 and 24 (South Mimms to Potters Bar), which was completed in September 1975. Yet back then this stretch of road was going to be numbered the M16, as part of the London Ringways scheme. In the end it became the A1178, which it remained for several years before being renumbered M25.

South of London the section between junctions 6 and 8 (Godstone to Reigate) opened in February 1976, initially as an east–west route to relieve the A25 – hence the number M25. Gradually more sections were added over the next ten years until the final section between Micklefield and South Mimms (junctions 19 to 23) was completed in October 1986. Two tunnels were also built on the M25 to the north of London. The Bell Common Tunnel, to the west of junction 27, goes under a cricket pitch and parts of Epping Forest, while the Holmfield Tunnel, to the east of junction 25, goes under a housing estate.

The actual start of the M25 motorway at junction 2 in Kent where it goes over the A2. (Wendy Chatterton)

One of two tunnels on the M25. This is the Bell Common Tunnel, near Epping in Essex, which goes under a cricket pitch and part of Epping Forest. (Wendy Chatterton)

By the time the M25 was formerly opened on 29 October 1986 by the prime minister, Margaret Thatcher, the M25 had become Britain's most expensive motorway to build, costing £909 million, working out at around £7.5 million per mile. Since then, at least the same amount has been spent on it, as no sooner than it was opened it needed upgrading. This was mainly to add extra lanes to cope with the amount of traffic using it and to turn it into a managed motorway in many parts. The main problem seemed to be the number of extra junctions that were added to the original scheme, which had envisaged the M25 as being a long-distance motorway. In fact, there were thirty-nine different public enquiries about the route of the M25, some of which resulted in extra junctions being added to its route, many of these only to local roads, causing extra local traffic to use it. On average it works out that there is a junction on the M25 less than every 4 miles.

As the M25 has become the busiest motorway on the motorway network, with over 200,000 vehicles a day using some sections, which is double the original estimate, it is hardly surprising that it became the first motorway in Britain to have a variable speed limit introduced. This happened in 1995 between junctions 10 (the A3) and 16 (the M4) originally as a trial, but from 1997 these became permanent. It also has the highest number of lanes on a single motorway carriageway – six between junctions 14 to 15, near Heathrow Airport. This section also had a massive 262,000 vehicles per day using it as recorded in 2014.

The widest section of lanes on a motorway in Britain. This is on the M25 south of junction 15 near Heathrow Airport, where each carriageway is six lanes wide. (Wendy Chatterton)

In the early days of the M25, with no speed cameras in place, some car drivers used the motorway as a racetrack, with organised events such as seeing how long it would take to do a complete circuit of the motorway. This was a common occurrence at weekends, with rumours of a lap of the motorway being completed in less than one hour, including a stop for the toll booths! The M25 has also been used at times, especially in the 1980s and 1990s, by partygoers on their way to illegal raves somewhere in London or the Home Counties.

Possibly the longest ever traffic jam on a British motorway is said to have happened on the M25 on 29 July 2012, when a clockwise queue of 49 miles was recorded, running from junction 19 (Watford) to junction 5 (Sevenoaks). A week earlier, on 22 July, there was a tailback of 26 miles reported between junction 8 (Reigate) and junction 16 (the M40). It is hardly surprising then that most of the M25 has now been turned into a smart motorway, with either all lane running or controlled motorway, apart from between junctions 4 and 5.

The M25 has been used as a location for several films and videos in popular culture over the years. The song *The Road to Hell* by Chris Rea is said to have been written about the M25. The 1987 film *Withnail and I* used an unopened section of the M25 for a scene when the main characters are seen driving along a motorway. The 2003 BBC docudrama *The Day Britain Stopped* had the M25 as the motorway where several accidents occurred.

One notable landmark is the Chalfont Viaduct, carrying the London Marylebone to Birmingham Moor Street railway line above the M25 to the north of junction 16 (the M40). The graffiti message 'Give Peas A Chance', a play on the John Lennon song, was visible for many years. It was finally removed in 2018. At one time there were often coach trips around the M25 pointing out the 'sights', complete with passengers receiving a certificate at the end of the trip.

An example of a four-stack junction on the M25, where the M1 and its slip roads go over the M25 at junction 21 in Hertfordshire. (Wendy Chatterton)

There are four service areas on the M25: Clackets Lane and Cobham in the south are directly connected with the carriageway, while South Mimms and Thurrock are accessed from junctions.

On its route, the M25 passes near to the following towns and cities: Dartford, Sevenoaks, Reigate, Epsom, Woking, Staines, Uxbridge, Watford, St Albans, Enfield, Romford and Brentwood. It is connected to the following motorways: the M1, M3, M4, M11, M20, M23, M26, M40 and A1 (M). It is also on the Euroroutes E15 and E30.

M26

This motorway links the M25 with the M20 in Kent, allowing traffic using the Channel Tunnel and the port of Dover convenient access from the south side of the M25, thus avoiding the Dartford Crossing. It is just under 10 miles (16 km) in length and known as 'the Wrotham Spur'. It starts at junction 3 of the M20 and continues to the M25 at junction 5. Traffic on the M26 going west must continue on the M25 to its next junction (6 for Godstone) before they can exit the motorway. This makes this the longest section of motorway in Britain between accessible junctions at 18 miles (29 km). It was opened in September 1980, joining up with some of the southern part of the M25 as far as junction 8 for Reigate. It was only in 1986 that the M25 was constructed north eastwards from

The M26 in Kent shortly after leaving the M25, looking east. (Wendy Chatterton)

junction 5 to join up with the A21 and continue to the Dartford Crossing. Its one and only junction is actually numbered '2A' due its closeness to junction 2 of the M20, which is slightly to the north.

M27

The M27 runs from the west of Southampton at Cadnam (junction 1) to the east side of Portsmouth at Hilsea, near junction 12. It is just under 28 miles (45 km) long. It was opened between the years 1973 and 1983. Originally it was designed to continue at least as far as Chichester in the east, but this didn't happen due to financial constraints. Instead, the A27 continues mainly as a dual carriageway to Lewes, west of Brighton. It also has two minor motorways leading south from it – the M271 into Southampton and the M275 into Portsmouth.

Although it was originally built as a three-lane motorway, several parts have now been widened to four lanes to cope with the traffic. The section between junctions 4 and 11 has been converted to a smart motorway, with hard shoulder running.

There are several unfinished parts of the motorway. There is no junction 6, as this was planned to take a spur, the M273, south into the Townhill Park area of Southampton. There was also an M272 proposed, which would link the M27 with the centre of Southampton. Instead, the A335 Thomas Lewis Way was built in a simpler form. A service area to the east of junction 9 never materialised either. So, there is just one service station – Rownhams services – which is to the east of the junction with the M271.

The M27 in Hampshire, looking west towards its junction with the M271.

M32

The M32 is a link motorway connecting the M4 with Bristol city centre, 4.4 miles (7.1 km) away. It was first opened as far back as September 1966 as the Hambrook Spur between junction 19 of the M4 and junction 1 of the M32, which connects to the A4174 Bristol Ring Road. The next section to junction 2 was opened by the Transport Minister, John Peyton, in July 1970. The final section, towards Bristol city centre via the A4032, which involved the demolition of several houses and businesses, opened in May 1975. Some of the section either side of junction 2 runs on an elevated part called the Eastville Viaduct, which has seen a 40-mph speed limit in place, due to its age.

It was proposed by Bristol City Council to downgrade the motorway to A road status, so that the hard shoulders could be used as a bus lane, but Highways England refused such a scheme. The motorway is mainly dual carriageway, apart from three lanes on the Hambrook Spur section between junctions 1 and 2. It is the only motorway in Britain numbered with a '30' number.

The M32 in Bristol, looking north from junction 3. Note the narrow hard shoulders.

M40

The M40 runs from Denham, north-west of London to its junction with the M42, near Solihull in the West Midlands. It is 89 miles (143 km) long and for several years was known as the 'London to Oxford motorway'. The first section to be opened was between junctions 4 and 5 near to High Wycombe in June 1967. Various other sections were added over the next few years including the Beaconsfield Bypass in 1971 and the Gerrards Cross Bypass in 1973. By March 1974 the motorway was opened as far as Wheatley a few miles east of Oxford and that is how it would stay for the next fifteen years.

The idea of extending it north to Birmingham was first mooted in the late 1960s, but it wasn't until 1987 that construction work began near Warwick. It was seen as an alternative route to Birmingham, with the M1 and M6 becoming increasingly clogged up. The route was planned to go through Otmoor, a semi-wetland landscape where several rare species of butterflies and birds were found, but after a high-profile protest the route was changed. The northern section, from Warwick to the M42, was opened in December 1989, while the southern section, from Oxford to Warwick, opened in January 1991.

One unusual feature on the M40 to the north of Banbury is where the carriageway splits into two parts and there is a section for a few miles where the central reservation is replaced with trees and bushes, with the safety barrier absent. Further south, near Stokenchurch, the motorway cuts through a chalk escarpment in the Chiltern Hills, known as Aston Rowant Cutting or the Stokenchurch Gap. It is shown in the opening credits to *The Vicar of Dibley* BBC TV comedy programme.

There are four service areas on the M40. These are Beaconsfield, Oxford, Cherwell Valley and Warwick services. Warwick was the first to be opened in 1994.

The M40 looking north between junctions 1A and 2, where there are four lanes of carriageway. (John Webb)

The iconic view from the Stokenchurch Gap on the M40, looking down into Oxfordshire, as shown in the opening credits for the *Vicar of Dibley*. (John Webb)

M42

The M42 goes mainly round the east and south of Birmingham, being part of a set of orbital motorways that circle round Britain's second city, known as the Birmingham Outer Ring Road. The northern terminus of the motorway is near the village of Measham in Leicestershire, but the road does continue as the A42 to reach the M1 at junction 23A. The southern end of the M42 is where it joins the M5 at Bromsgrove in Worcestershire. It is 40 miles (64.4 km) in length.

It was designed to link up with the M6 and the M5, so that there would be a ring of motorways around Birmingham. The first section to open was the link from the M6 to Birmingham Airport in November 1976. The final section from Bromsgrove to the M5 was opened in December 1989, over twenty years after the first section. Originally the motorway was planned to link up with the M1 near Nottingham, but instead a trunk road, the A42 link, was constructed in 1989 to bridge this gap. The M42 also links up with the end of the M40 at junction 3A to the south-east of Birmingham.

The M42 was the first motorway in Britain to experiment with 'hard shoulder running', whereby the hard shoulder was used as an extra lane to cope with heavy traffic. This was introduced in 2006 along with variable speed limits under the Active Traffic Management system. This was between junctions 3a and 7, and due to its success in lowering journey times it was extended to junction 9 in the north and to junction 15 in the south.

When the M6 Toll motorway was built in 2003 it used part of the M42 for its route between junctions 7A and 9. There are two sets of services on the motorway – one at Hopwood Park, near Redditch in the south, and one at Tamworth in the north – though there have been plans to build a third one near to the NEC and Birmingham Airport.

Looking up to junction 4, near Solihull, on the M42 in the West Midlands. Note that this section is designated a 'smart motorway', though at the time the hard shoulder was not being used by traffic.

M45

The M45 runs from junction 17 of the M1, near Daventry, to its end at its junction with the A45 to the south of Rugby. It is just under 8 miles (12.7 km) long and is one of the least used motorways in Britain. It is also one of the oldest stretches of motorway in Britain, being opened in November 1959 – at the same time as the M1 and the M10. It was built at the northern end of the M1 as a way of spreading the traffic flow away from the single terminus of the M1 with the A5 at junction 18, near Crick in Northamptonshire. This meant that traffic for Coventry and the southern parts of Birmingham could leave the M1 at junction 17 and go along the M45 and help ease possible congestion at junction 18. The M45 still has some of its original concrete bridges from the 1950s and is dual carriageway throughout. It has just one junction, which was added to the M45 in 1991. With the opening of the M6 from Rugby to Birmingham in 1972 and the M40 in 1991, traffic going to and from Birmingham has tended to avoid the M45.

One of the oldest motorways in Britain, the M45 is also one of the quietest, as illustrated in this photograph of a deserted motorway. (Wendy Chatterton)

M48

The M48 is the original M4 motorway, which went over the first Severn Bridge. It runs from the M4 (junction 21) at Thornbury in England to the M4 (junction 23) at Caldicot in Wales. It is 13 miles (20.9 km) in length and one of only three cross-border motorways in Britain. It was opened as the M4 in 1966 and saved traffic between England and Wales having to go all the way north to Gloucester to cross the River Severn. After a significant increase in traffic, a report commissioned in 1984 suggested constructing a second Severn crossing to the south. This finally opened in September 1996, with the M4 using this more direct route, leading to this section of motorway being designated the M48.

It has one services, Severn View services, by junction 1 where a footpath leads onto the bridge so pedestrians and cyclists are able to cross the bridge, which is unusual, since pedestrians and cyclists are normally banned from motorways.

The bridge had a toll charge from its opening in 1966 until it was abolished in 2018. There is also a second river crossing on this stretch of the M48, namely the Wye Bridge to the west of the Severn Bridge. This is the river that marks the boundary between England and Wales, rather than the River Severn itself.

The one crowning glory of the former M4, which has been renumbered M48, is the original Severn Bridge, pictured here looking north.

M49

The M49 is a 5-mile (8.0 km) link motorway between the M4 (junction 22) and the M5 (junction 18A) and is situated to the north-west of Bristol. It saves motorists having to use the Almondsbury Interchange several miles to the east to transfer from the M4 to the M5 and vice-versa.

It was built at the same time as new M4 Severn Crossing, opening in June 1996. It is unusual in that for many years it could only be accessed from the M4 or the M5, as opposed to a non-motorway road. Since August 2020 a new junction – junction 1 – has been in place that links the motorway to the A403. However, at the time of writing the junction is not in use due to a dispute as to who will finance the building of the connecting road to the junction, which has yet to be constructed.

The M49 is a short spur connecting the M4 and M5 motorways north-west of Bristol, seen here looking north to its junction with the M4.

M50

This was one of the first motorways to be built and has changed little since it first opened in November 1960. It runs from the M5 at junction 8 to Ross-on-Wye in Herefordshire, where it joins up with the A40, A449 and A465 roads. It is just over 21.5 miles (34.8 km) in length and may be described as being 'quaint' in that it hasn't changed that much over the years. One unusual feature of it is at junction 3, which goes onto the B4221. Known as the 'Linton Interchange', it is basically a T-junction with hardly any time to slow down if you leave the motorway here. The M50 crosses the River Severn and its flood plain on the Queenhill Bridge and Viaduct.

The reason for it being built in the first place was to provide a fast, direct link between South Wales and the West Midlands, as the only alternative was the A449, which went to the west of Wolverhampton, or the heavily congested A38. It was originally called 'the Ross Spur motorway' after the name of the town where it terminated. In fact, most of it was opened before the M5, which it was eventually connected to. So, junctions 1 to 4 opened in 1960, while junction 1 to the M50 opened in 1962 at the same time as the M5 in this area. There are no actual services on the motorway, though Strensham services are situated at its junction with the M5.

One of the strangest junctions on Britain's motorway network is found on the M50 in Herefordshire. This is junction 3 for the B4221, which is essentially a T-junction with very little deceleration lane available. (Wendy Chatterton)

M53

The M53 was originally a motorway from Wallasey on the Wirral to junction 5 on the A41, just south of Eastham, known as the 'Mid Wirral motorway'. This section was opened in February 1972 by Lord Leverhulme in a ceremony at the southern end of the M53. There were plans to extend it south to Backford, near Chester, as shown by the wide curve, called the 'Hooton Fork', just to the west of junction 5. Instead, the motorway was joined up with the M531, 'the Ellesmere Port motorway', which had been opened in December 1975 as a northern bypass for the town of Ellesmere Port. The M531 was then incorporated into the M53 in March 1981, when a viaduct over the A5117 roundabout was opened. At the eastern end of the motorway junctions 10 to 11 were opened in 1981, joining the M53 to the M56. Finally, the motorway to junction 12 was opened in 1982 joining it with the A55 North Wales Expressway, giving it a total length of 18.9 miles (30.4 km).

The northern terminus of the M53 at junction 1 leads onto the A59, which in turn connects with the Wallasey or Kingsway Tunnel to Liverpool. So, the motorway gives an alternative route to and from Liverpool via the Wirral. At its northern end, Bidston Viaduct has been strengthened twice – in 1998/9 and in 2012 – to cope with heavier HGVs using it. The motorway has its own spur south of Bidston, which goes west to Moreton.

The M53 on the Wirral Peninsula looking north. This section was opened in 1973 and leads to the Wallasey Tunnel and ultimately Liverpool. (Howard Johnston)

M54

The M54 is a motorway that runs east to west from the M6 (junction 10A) north of Wolverhampton in the West Midlands to Wellington, near Shrewsbury, Shropshire. The road then continues as the A5 trunk road, which goes on to Holyhead in North Wales. It is 23 miles (37 km) long and was first opened in 1975 as the 'Wellington Bypass' with the number A5(M). The rest of the motorway was constructed in four different stages by four different contractors and was finally completed in 1983.

The main problem with the M54 is its junction with the M6. Traffic going from the M54 onto the M6 can only go to the south, so traffic wishing to use the M6 northbound or the M6 Toll has to come off at junction 1. There have been plans to rectify this problem, including the possible demolition of the Hilton Park services, but at the time of writing nothing definite has been put into place. There is one service station at Telford, just off junction 4 of the motorway.

The M54, looking westwards between junctions 2 and 3, near Wolverhampton. (Wendy Chatterton)

M55

The M55 takes traffic from the M6 at junction 32, near Preston, to Blackpool, just over 12 miles (19.6 km) away. It helps relieve congestion in Preston and the roads leading to and from Blackpool – one of Britain's biggest seaside resorts. The first section to be opened was between the M6 and junction 1 in 1958, as it was part of Britain's first ever motorway, the Preston Bypass. It wasn't until 1975 that the rest of the motorway was opened between Junctions 1 and 4. There is no junction 2 on the M55 as this was to be the junction where the Preston Western Bypass leading from the M65 would join the motorway. Plans for this were dropped in the 1990s. However, in 2013 Preston City Council and Lancashire County Council agreed to build a Preston Western Distributor Road, which will link the A583 and A584 to a new junction 2 of the M55. Construction started in 2019 with an expected completion date of 2023.

Just before the motorway was opened in 1975 a strange event took place. This was the landing and take-off of a Jaguar jet fighter from the nearby British Aircraft Corporation site at Wharton. A large crowd gathered to witness this unique event, which was designed to show the capabilities of this jet fighter in situations where it might have to land or take off in a limited space – in this case a motorway. There is footage of the event on YouTube.

The M55 links Blackpool with the M6 and the rest of the motorway network. This view is looking east towards the Pennine Hills, just before junction 5 for Kirkham. (Ian Park)

M56

The M56 runs from junction 4 of the M60 in south Manchester in a south-westerly direction to the north of Chester in Cheshire. It is 33.3 miles (53.6 km) long and provides a route across north and west Cheshire from Manchester to North Wales, where it joins up with the A494 and then the A55. On its route it provides links with the M6 (junctions 20/20A) at junction 9, and the M53 (junction 15) at junction 11.

The motorway first opened in 1971 between junctions 11 and 14. Then the eastern part of it between junctions 1 and 11 was opened in stages between 1972 and 1975. Finally, a western extension to junction 16 was opened in 1981. However, this junction ended at a small roundabout on the A5117, which was not ideal, and so in the 2000s a free-flowing junction onto the A494 was built to make the road continuous without any breaks.

Sometimes known as the 'North Cheshire motorway', the M53 has junction 13 missing from its route, though most people can only speculate as to the reason why. Apart from 13 being an unlucky number, the land to the north here is mainly marshland, though the Stanlow Oil Refinery and other industrial complexes are nearby. So, this could be the stimulus for a possible future access road to them. The M56 is part of Euroroute E22.

Looking west along the M56 near Ellesmere Port, towards the Clywdian Hills of North Wales and the end of the motorway.

M57

The M57, also known as 'the Liverpool Outer Ring Road', is a motorway that bypasses parts of Liverpool from the south-east to the north-west. It is 10 miles (16 km) in length and originally was planned to run from the A562 near Widnes in the south to the A565 near Southport in the north. Many people consider it an unfinished motorway as it doesn't go completely round the eastern edge of Liverpool.

The motorway starts at its interchange with junction 6 of the M62 at Tarbock and ends at junction 7, the notorious Switch Island junction. Here the M57 meets the start of the M58, the A59, the A5036 and the A578. It was meant to have a flyover carrying the M57 above it, but this never happened and so it has been remodelled on more than one occasion, though long queues are still quite common here.

The M57 was opened in two stages: Phase 1 for junctions 4 to 7 in 1972, and Phase 2 for junctions 1 to 4 in 1974. A southern extension was linked to the M57 in the 1990s taking it to the A562, with its connections to Widnes and south Liverpool, but it never become part of the M57. Instead, it was a dual carriageway, numbered the A5300 and called the Knowsley Expressway. Similarly, in 2015 a new road, the A5758, was built to the north of the M57, linking it to the A565 and Southport, effectively completing the Liverpool Outer Ring Road.

The M57 cuts across the eastern edge of Liverpool and is a useful bypass route for lorries going to and from Liverpool Docks – hence the information on the sign. (Wendy Chatterton)

M58

The M58 runs from Switch Island Junction, near Aintree, north of Liverpool, to the M6 (junction 26), near Wigan – 12 miles (19.3 km) away. It was built both to provide a fast route to the M6 for traffic using the Liverpool Docks, as well as for linking the new town of Skelmersdale with both Liverpool and Wigan. It was originally opened in 1968 as the Skelmersdale Regional Road (A506), between junctions 4 and 5. This section was later upgraded from a two-lane single carriageway to dual carriageway in 1973. The section from here to the M6 (junctions 5 to 6) was opened in 1970 as a dual carriageway, but was upgraded to three lanes with a hard shoulder in 1977. This is when this road became the M58. Finally, the remaining part of today's M58 between Switch Island and junction 4 was opened in 1980.

There have been several plans to extend the motorway at either end. A section east of the M6 to Bolton had been suggested and there was even a bridge built over this proposed section on the M61. At the western end the motorway was possibly going to go down towards Liverpool city centre as a relief road for the A59. The A5036 dual carriageway provides a fast link to the docks at Bootle though traffic still has to negotiate the often-congested Switch Island Junction.

Finally, there is no junction 2 on the motorway. This should have been built to connect a proposed 'M59' from this motorway to the M55, west of Preston.

Another motorway used by docks traffic from Liverpool is the M58, which is joined to the M6 at its eastern end. This view is looking eastwards and is near junction 5 for Skelmersdale. (Wendy Chatterton)

M60

The M60, Manchester Outer Ring Road or Manchester Ring Motorway, is an orbital motorway that surrounds most of Manchester. It is 36.1 miles (58.1 km) in length and was built over a forty-year period starting in 1960. It has swallowed up several other motorways in its evolution, including the M62, the M63, the M66 and the M68, and was named the M60 in 1998, being finally completed in 2000. For 7 miles (11 km) it shares the same route as the M62 between junctions 12 and junctions 18, which skirts across the north-western part of Manchester.

Junction 1 is at Stockport in the south and, going round the motorway in a clockwise direction, it connects with no fewer than six other motorways – the M56, the M62, the M602, the M61, the M66 and the M67. The motorway has twenty-seven junctions, giving it an average of just 1.3 miles (2.1 km) between them – the lowest average distance on any motorway in Britain. This may help to explain why there are no services on the M60.

The first section of the M60 to be opened was the M62 Stretford to Eccles Bypass in 1960, though this was renumbered as the M63 in 1971. This was followed by the openings of the M62, the M63, the M66 and the M68 at various points around Manchester between 1974 and 1989. Parts of, or all of, these had their numbers changed to the M60 in 1998. The final section of the M60 to be opened was between junctions 19 and 24 in October 2000.

It has at times been the busiest motorway in Britain, with an average of 181,000 vehicles per day recorded in 2004 using the section between junctions 16 and 17 – nicknamed 'Death Valley' by locals. A large section of the M60 is now designated a smart motorway – from junction 8 to junction 18. It is part of the Euroroutes E20 and E22.

The M60 Manchester orbital motorway goes round Manchester in a complete circle, though the section shown here is shared with the M62. This view, just to the west of the Simister Interchange (junction 18), is one of the busiest sections of motorway in Britain.

M61

The M61 is a 22-mile (36 km) motorway that runs from the M60/M62 north-west of Manchester to the M6 and M65 motorways near Preston. It was opened in stages between February 1969 and December 1970. It helps traffic going from Manchester to Blackpool and the Lake District avoid the M6 and M62 for part of their journey.

The first section of the M61 to be opened in November 1969 was the section between Bolton and Preston – junction 4 to the M6 at junction 30. The following year, in December 1970, the rest of the motorway was opened from the M62 to junction 4. This section includes the renowned Worsley Braided Interchange in Greater Manchester, where the M60 and the M61 motorways meet along with several local roads. It is a massive seventeen lanes wide at Linnyshaw Moss, which has merited a place in the *Guinness World Records* for having the highest number of lanes next to each other in Britain. In its early days it was actually called 'Spaghetti Junction' by locals well before that name was given to the Gravelly Hill Interchange on the M6 in Birmingham.

Although the M61 is connected to the M60 at junction 15, the M61 itself runs onto the A580, the East Lancashire Road, which some say is really the unsigned A666 (M). Further north the motorway bypasses the towns of Bolton, Horwich and Chorley, following more or less the route of the A6. The M61 has one service station at Rivington between junctions 6 and 8, which opened in August 2011. It replaced the much-criticised Bolton West services, at one time deemed the worst service station in Great Britain on the Motorways Services website.

There is one mystery connected with the M61, and that is the fact that it does not have a junction 7. It may have been earmarked as a junction for Chorley South, but for whatever reason it was never built. There are two notable landmarks that can be seen from the motorway. Firstly, near Horwich is the Pennine outcrop of Rivington Moor, which dominates the skyline to the east. Then, at Chorley, by junction 8, is the Preston England Temple, belonging to the Church of the Latter-day Saints. It is made of white marble, and at night the church is floodlit so it is easily seen for miles around.

The M61, looking south, near junction 3. Shortly after this is the largest number of roadways running together in Britain, at the Worsley Braided Interchange. (Wendy Chatterton)

M62

The M62 runs across northern England from Liverpool in the west, passing the north of Manchester, cutting through the Pennine Hills before passing south of Bradford and Leeds, and finally terminating to the west of Hull in the east. It is 107 miles (172 km) in length, though since 2000 it has shared 7 miles (11 km) of its route with the M60 Orbital Motorway near Manchester, between junctions 12 (Eccles) and 18 (Simister). The road signs in this section have the same junction numbers for both motorways. For several years there was a motorway numbered the M62 around the south-west Manchester area, but this became the M63 (and eventually the M60) once the current M62 was constructed.

The M62 was officially opened by the Queen on 14 October 1971, though this was only a small section of the motorway across the Pennines near Huddersfield. It would be another five years until the motorway was finally completed. This section of the M62 was one of the hardest motorways to build, partly due to the difficult terrain and partly due to frequent bad weather.

The final section from junctions 4 to 6 on the eastern edge of Liverpool was finished in November 1976 – six years after construction first began. The reason why the M62 starts at junction 4 and not junction 1 as you would expect is because originally it was intended to build the motorway into Liverpool via a long tunnel, terminating near Lime Street station in the city centre, but due to costs and the need to rehouse many people this never happened.

The M62 is Britain's highest motorway, reaching a height of 1,221 feet (372 metres) near junction 22 at Windy Hill on Saddleworth Moor, on the western side of the Pennines. It is also Britain's lowest motorway, reaching a height of just 2 metres above sea level near Goole at its eastern end.

Due to its proximity between several large metropolitan areas, the M62 is one of the worst motorways for congestion in Britain, with an average daily traffic flow of around 144,000 vehicles recorded around the Bradford/Leeds area in 2008. To help with traffic flow the M62 has been turned into a smart motorway in three sections, between junctions 10–12, junctions 18–20, and junctions 25–30.

The M62, looking west near Manchester where it shares the same route as the M60. This is known as a 'multiplex' among road enthusiasts.

There is a famous urban myth about the M62 where the motorway divides into two separate carriageways as it goes around Stott Hall Farm between junctions 22 and 23. Some people think the farmer refused to move out when the motorway was being built, so they had to build the motorway around the farm instead. The real reason was that the ground where the motorway should have gone had weak peat bogs, so if the motorway had gone in a straight line through the farm it could have resulted in the carriageway sinking into the soft ground. Either side of the farm the ground was much firmer, so this is why it splits in two here. This feature of the M62 made it into a top 10 of 'Best Motorway Views' in 2007.

Other notable features of the motorway include the Scammonden Bridge, which carries the B6114 over the motorway between junctions 22 and 23; the Ouse Bridge between junction 36 and 37, which carries the M62 over the River Ouse near Goole; Simister Island Interchange (junction 18), where the M60 leaves the M62 to go south and where the M66 starts from; and the Lofthouse Interchange at junction 29, where the M1 meets the M62.

The motorway has seen several notable incidents since it was first opened. On the night of 1–2 March 2018 during the notorious 'Beast from the East' white out over Britain, around 3,500 vehicles became trapped on the M62 eastbound between junctions 20 and 24 over the top of the Pennines. A Highways England car had caught fire in extreme weather conditions causing the motorway to become blocked. Around 200 of those caught up in the blockage had to stay in their vehicles overnight until the motorway was cleared.

The famous Stott Hall Farm on the M62 between junctions 22 and 23, looking west, where the carriageway splits considerably as it goes past the farm to avoid the soft ground here. (Photo © Peter McDermott (cc-b-sa/2.0)

IN
MEMORY OF
THOSE WHO TRAGICALLY
LOST THEIR LIVES AS A RESULT
OF THE M62 COACH BOMB
FEBRUARY 4th 1974

4th Light Regt RA
BDR Terence Griffin   Aged 24
GNR Leonard Godden   Aged 22
5th Sig Regt
SGMN Michael Eugene Waugh   Aged 32
SGMN Leslie David Walsh   Aged 17
11th Sig Regt
SGMN Paul Anthony Reid   Aged 17
2nd Bn RRF
LCPL James John McShane   Aged 28
FUS Jack Thomas Hynes   Aged 19
FUS Stephen Whalley   Aged 18
CPL Clifford Haughton   Aged 23
Wife
Mrs Linda Haughton   Aged 23
(Nee Malone)
Children
Lee Haughton   Aged 5
Robert Haughton   Aged 2

"IN OUR HEARTS AND MINDS
THEY WILL LIVE ON FOREVER"

Marshalls
natural stone

The memorial to the victims of the terrorist bombing on the M62 at Harsthead Moor services.

The M62 also saw the first and only terrorist attack on a British motorway, when a bomb in a coach carrying RAF personnel and their families was detonated by terrorists on 4 February 1974. It happened between junction 26 (Chain Bar) and junction 27 (Gildersome). Twelve passengers were killed, and thirty-eight others injured. A memorial to the victims is situated at the Hartshead Moor services between junctions 25 and 26.

There are four service areas on the M62. They are Burtonwood, Birch, Hartshead Moor and Ferrybridge going from west to east. The M62 passes near to the towns and cities of Liverpool, Warrington, Manchester, Rochdale, Oldham, Halifax, Huddersfield, Bradford, Leeds, Wakefield, Pontefract and Goole. It is connected to the following motorways: M1, M6, M18, M57, M60, M61, M66, M602, M606, M621, A1 (M) and A627 (M). It is also part of the Euroroutes E20 and E22.

M65

The M65 is a motorway in Lancashire that connects Preston in the west with Burnley and Colne in the east. It is 25.8 miles (41.5 km) long and was opened in different stages between the years 1981 and 1997. The motorway finished at junction 6 to the east of Blackburn from 1984 until the western extension linking it to the M61 and the M6 was opened in 1997. Originally the motorway was planned to go through Blackburn as an urban motorway, but opposition caused the route to go south of the city.

Some hope to see the motorway as one day becoming a second trans-Pennine motorway as a rival to the M62, with the eastern end going over the Pennines and into Leeds. The western end was planned to go round the south and west of Preston and join with the M55 at junction 2 of that motorway. To date this hasn't happened, though the Preston Distributor Road is currently being built from the M55 to the A583, but not as far round to the M65.

The hilly nature of the M65 is apparent here as it climbs a hill westbound shortly before its junction with the M61 south of Preston. (Carol Park)

M66

The M66 is a motorway in Greater Manchester and Lancashire that runs from the M60 (junction 18) in the south to just north of Ramsbottom, Lancashire, in the north. It is 8 miles (12.9 km) long and originally went further south towards Stockport. This southern section from the Simister Interchange (junction 4) to Denton became the M60 in 1998 and so the M66 became much shorter. Interestingly the M66 is numbered from the north so it actually begins near Ramsbottom and ends at Simister, at junction 18 of the M60/M62.

Another hilly motorway, also in Lancashire, is the M66, seen here near its northern end at Ramsbottom. (Wendy Chatterton)

Part of the motorway is a bypass of the town of Bury, though it does pass right through the middle of a post-war housing estate at Ferngrove in Bury, where an area of green playing field was used for the M66. There are high walls to cut down the noise, but it is still very noisy for local residents as it is a on a hill. The M66 was hoped to have gone further north to join up with the M65 near Burnley, but instead it changes into the A65 dual carriageway.

M67

The M67 is a motorway in the Greater Manchester area that runs eastwards from the M60 (junction 24) to Hattersely at junction 4. It passes through the towns of Denton and Hyde on its 5-mile-long (8.0 km) route. It was originally going to join up the A57 (M) in central Manchester to the M1 near Sheffield, and as such was seen as an alternative trans-Pennine motorway to the M62 further north. In fact, at either end of the M57 there are road stumps where the motorway would have continued. At its eastern end traffic wishing to continue further east across the Pennines can either take the A628, or the A616 to the M1 at junction 35A, or go further south via the A57 'Snake Pass' route into Sheffield. Both routes are very slow and full of curves, so a lot of the traffic going across the Pennines to Sheffield tends to go via the M60, the M62 and the M1 instead.

The proposed M57 motorway further east of the current M57 would have used some of the route of the former Woodhead Railway between Hadfield and Stocksbridge, using the

The M67 is one of several motorways that were never completed as hoped. It is seen here looking eastwards towards the Pennines. (Wendy Chatterton)

Woodhead Tunnel for one carriageway. At Stocksbridge on the Yorkshire side, the current Stocksbridge Bypass on the A616 has used the alignment of the proposed M57, but this has not been built to motorway standards.

More recently plans have been put forward for a long tunnel underneath the Peak District to take the M57 to Sheffield. These were changed in 2017 to having a mixture of open road and tunnel due to escalating costs.

M69

The M69 is a three-lane motorway between Coventry in Warwickshire and Leicester in Leicestershire. It is 15.7 miles (25.3 km) long and was built to link the East and West Midlands as an alternative route to the A46. It runs in a north-easterly direction from junction 2 of the M6, near Coventry, to junction 21 of the M1, near Leicester. It was opened in 1977 and was originally known as the 'Coventry–Leicester motorway'. Prior to it being constructed there was a local campaign group, known as M69 Now, who campaigned for the motorway to be built.

At its southern end, the motorway splits in two with a direct link onto the M6 and another direct link onto the A46 Coventry Bypass. At its northern end the motorway could have gone over the M1 via a flyover and connect with the A563 Leicester Outer Ring Road, but there was opposition to this and it was never built. However, the infrastructure is in place should direct slip roads onto the M1 ever be built. There were also plans to extend the motorway south, around Coventry to join up with the M5 and M50 at Strensham, but like a lot of motorway schemes this never happened.

A useful link motorway that joins the M1 with the M6. The M69 is seen here in Warwickshire looking north. (Wendy Chatterton)

M73

The M73 links the M74 near Uddingston in south-east Glasgow to the M80, near Mollinsburn in Scotland. It is a useful motorway for traffic going north to south across the Central Belt, avoiding Glasgow in the process. It is quite short at just 7 miles (11.3 km) long, yet it links to three different motorways – the M8, the M74 and the M80. It was opened between May 1971 and April 1972, with the northern end extended to the M80 in 2011.

When the 'missing link' of the M8 between Baillieston and Chappelhall was finally opened in April 2017 the upgraded Baillieston Interchange helped to connect the two motorways. The junction at 2A for Gartcosh was opened in 1999. It is unusual in that it is accessed from a minor road rather than the A752, which crosses the motorway half a mile further south.

The M73, seen here at Gartcosh, links the M74, M8 and M80 motorways to the east of Glasgow, helping traffic avoid having to going through the city. (Allan Heron)

M74

The M74 links with the M8 at junctions 20/21 in south Glasgow with the A74 (M) at junction 13, Abington services in the Southern Uplands of Scotland. It is a continuous motorway with the A74(M) with its junctions numbered 1 to 22, though the motorway has two different numbers.

The M74 is 40 miles (64 km) long. and was built in three different parts, with the first section, the Hamilton Bypass, from junctions 5 to 8 (Hamilton to Larkhall South), being opened by Willie Ross, the Secretary of State for Scotland on 2 December 1966. Other sections were opened between 1968 and 1991.

It was expected that the whole motorway to the English border would become the M6, but instead it was numbered the A74 (M) south of Abington in 1999. Finally, the section north of Uddingston to the M8, 'the M74 Completion', was finally opened in June 2011, in spite of a lot of opposition. This is one of the last pieces of new motorway to be opened in Britain, apart from the missing link of the M8 in 2017.

There are three services on the M74 – at Abington, Bothwell and Hamilton. There is another services, Cairn Lodge, near Happenden, which is next to the M74 and is accessed from junction 11 or 12 depending on the direction you are travelling in.

View of junction 4 of the M74 westbound, near Glasgow, where the M73 begins. (Allan Heron)

M77

The M77 is a motorway that links the south of Glasgow (starting at junction 22 of the M8) to Fenwick, near Kilmarnock in Scotland. It is 20 miles (32.2 km long) and was originally planned to go as far as Ayr on the coast. It was built as an alternative route for the large amount of commuter traffic from the Glasgow suburbs and heavy goods traffic from the port of Stranraer, which used the A77 into Glasgow.

When the first section of the M77 opened in October 1977 it was only a short 1.5-mile-long (2.4 km) motorway that went as far as the B768 Dumbreck Road near to Bellahouston Park in the Glasgow suburbs. It would be nearly twenty years before the next section was opened in April 1996, taking the motorway through the south western suburbs of Glasgow as far as junction 3 at Arden. Several months later in December 1996 the M77 reached junction 5 to the south of Newton Mearns, where it stayed that way for almost ten years. The final section opened in April 2005 which was 9 miles (14.5 km) in length and ran to the motorway's present terminus at junction 8 near Fenwick, where the road continues as the A77 to Kilmarnock and beyond.

The M77, looking north from the B762, south-west of Glasgow. (Allan Heron)

M80

The M80 is a motorway that links the M8 from the north-east of Glasgow to the M9, south of Stirling. It is an important route as it connects Glasgow and the south of Scotland with the Highlands to the north of Stirling. It is 25 miles (40.2 km) long and parts of it were known as the 'Stepps Bypass' at one time.

It was opened in three different stages between the years 1974 and 2011. The first section to be opened in May 1974 was between the village of Haggs and the A9 south of Stirling. The second section between the M8 at junction 13 to the other side of Stepps opened in June 1992 as the Stepps Bypass. The final section between Stepps and Haggs was finally opened in September 2011, allowing the M80 to join up with the M9 at Bannockburn.

There is just one set of services on the M80 at junction 8 which are shared with the M9 and known as Stirling services. It is one of the smallest motorway service areas in Britain. The M80 is connected to the M8, M9, M73 and M876.

View of the M80 southbound carriageway near junction 1 where it joins with the M8. (Allan Heron)

M90

The M90 runs from junction 1A of the M9 to the west of Edinburgh, crossing over the Firth of Forth at the Queensferry Crossing on its route north, and ends at Perth where it splits into two branches. It is 36 miles (58 km) long and is the most northerly motorway in Great Britain. It was opened at different times north of the Forth between the years 1964 and 1980. The section south of the Forth was opened between 2007 and 2017, some it originally being a spur of the M9.

The motorway originally started north of the Forth Road Bridge, but with the opening of the Queensferry Crossing bridge in August 2017, the M90 was extended south to join up with the M9. The Queensferry Crossing is one of two bridges on the M90 and is 1.7 miles (2.7 km) in length. It was built to replace the Forth Road Bridge, where structural issues were found in 2004.

The other bridge on the motorway is the Friarton Bridge near Perth, and is approached from the south on a tight curve. Soon after the bridge the M90 splits into two different branches of the same motorway. The eastern branch goes on to join up with the A90 at junction 11 for traffic going north east to Dundee and Aberdeen. This motorway was originally numbered as the M85 as it was joined to the A85. When the route to Aberdeen was renumbered A90, the M85 became the M90 to tie in with this renumbering. The western branch goes round the western side of Perth and ends at junction 12 where it joins up with the A9 for traffic going northwards to Inverness and Thurso.

The M90 passes near to the towns of Inverkeithing, Dunfermline and Cowdenbeath. It has a short spur, the A823 (M), linking it with Dunfermline. It is part of the Euroroute E15.

The M90 crosses the Firth of Forth on the Queensferry Crossing, which opened in 2017, replacing the Forth Road Bridge.

The M90, looking north on the north side of the Queensferry Crossing in Fife. (Wendy Chatterton)

M180

The M180 motorway in north Lincolnshire links junction 5 of the M18 near Doncaster North services to the A180 at Barnetby. Here the A180 continues on to Grimsby with links to the port of Immingham on the Humber. It also has links to the Humber Bridge and the port of Hull via the A15. The motorway was opened in stages between the years 1977 and 1979, partly as a bypass for the towns of Brigg and Scunthorpe, and partly to carry freight traffic between the Humber ports and the rest of the country.

View along the M180 in Lincolnshire, one of the flattest motorways in Britain. (Wendy Chatterton)

It is 25.5 miles (41 km) long and despite its strategic importance was only given a three-digit motorway number rather than a two-digit number beginning with a 1. It has a spur off it to Scunthorpe, the M181, and is one of the flattest motorways in Britain. It is also part of Euroroute E22.

M181

This is a short 2-mile (3.2 km) motorway that links the western end of Scunthorpe to junction 3 of the M180 motorway in Lincolnshire. It was opened in December 1978 and runs more or less straight over flat land. Its purpose was to join Scunthorpe and the steelworks in the town to the motorway network. It is a two-lane motorway with hard shoulders and its future as a motorway is now uncertain. This is because of the Lincolnshire

The M181, near Scunthorpe, is one of the shortest motorways in Britain, whose days are numbered due to it likely being downgraded in the next few years. (Wendy Chatterton)

Lakes Development where a huge housing development is being built on either side of the motorway. To access this development the motorway has had a new roundabout built roughly halfway along its length at a junction with the B1450. It is anticipated that the northern part of the M181 will become the A1077, while the southern part will be a slip road connecting to the M180.

M271

The M271 motorway starts at the A36 in the district of Redbridge in Southampton and proceeds north out of Southampton for 3 miles (4.8 km) to join up with the A3057 near the village of Upton. This road continues to the town of Romsey and further on to Salisbury.

It is an unusual motorway because at junction 2 with the M27 (junction 3) there is an at-grade roundabout with traffic signals before the motorway continues either side of this junction. It is a useful route for traffic coming to and from Southampton Western Docks avoiding Southampton town centre. It is frequently congested on some Saturdays with cruise traffic and in the rush hour at its southern end where it meets the A35.

Looking south on the M271 towards Southampton, with stationery traffic on the northbound carriageway caused by the roundabout at junction 3 with the M27. (Wendy Chatterton)

M275

This motorway links the city of Portsmouth in Hampshire from the A3 to the M27. It is just 2 miles (3.2 km) in length and was opened in 1976. Unusually for motorways, it comes under the jurisdiction of Portsmouth City Council rather than Highways England.

There was an unfinished junction for the Tipner area of Portsmouth, which wasn't completed due it being less than 1.25 miles (2.01 km) from the next junction. In 2005, plans for this junction were reintroduced and it was only in 2014 that this junction finally opened as junction 1 and the original junction 1 was renamed junction 2.

The local landmark, the *Sails of the South* can be found between the two carriageways of the motorway. This is a 141-foot-high (43 m) structure of three sails from a sailing boat, which were built as part of the regeneration scheme known as the Tipner Gateway Project.

Looking north along the M275 as it leaves Portsmouth to join with the M27. The structure in the central reservation is called the *Sails of the South* (or *Trimast*).

M602

The M602 is a short 4-mile (6.4 km) motorway that runs from junction 12 of the M60/M62, at Worsley, to Ordsall in Salford where it continues as the A57 into central Manchester.

This motorway has undergone several number changes over the years. It was originally going to be called the M52, linking Liverpool and Manchester. It would be known as the South Lancashire motorway and would link with the national motorway network through a connection with the M6. However, the M62 Trans-Pennine motorway, connecting the west coast of England with the east coast, became more of a priority and so the western section of the M52 became part of the M62, leaving a 4-mile stretch from Worsley to Salford remaining. It was renumbered the M64 first and then the M602.

The first section of the M602 from Worsley to Eccles was opened in November 1971, while the second section from Eccles to Ordsall was opened in December 1982. At its eastern end it runs onto the A57, which runs eastward to the Mancunian Way, the A57(M), bypassing the southern edge of Manchester city centre. At one time there were tentative plans to continue the M602 right through central Manchester to Sheffield in the east. The M57 east of Manchester is the only part of this motorway and runs to the edge of the Pennines.

The start of the M602 as it leaves the M62 west of Manchester. It is one of the straightest pieces of motorway in Britain. (Wendy Chatterton)

M606

The M606 is a short spur leading from junction 26 of the M62, the Chain Bar Interchange, towards the centre of Bradford. The motorway was opened in 1972–73 and is just 3 miles (4.8 km) in length. It is sometimes called the 'Bradford Spur motorway', and when it was first opened it had the number A638 (M).

The northern end of the motorway is unusual for several reasons. Originally the motorway ended at the Staygate roundabout, going on to the A6177 eastbound and A6036 westbound. Then in 1999 a new slip road was built so eastbound traffic could access the motorway at ground level directly from the A6177 to the west of the motorway. This junction was changed again in 2004 so traffic coming off the motorway could go under the Staygate roundabout and then turn right only onto the A6177. It is now a T-junction of sorts, with traffic lights there to direct the flow of traffic. As a result, there are now two junctions numbered 1 on the M606.

From 2008 to 2009 the M606 had a HOV lane whereby vehicles carrying two or more people were allowed to use this lane. The motorway is officially called the Bradford South Radial Motorway.

The northern terminus of the M606 in Bradford, West Yorkshire. Note the unusual junction layout with traffic exiting the motorway to the right, while traffic can only enter from the left.

M621

This motorway links the southern edge of Leeds city centre with two different motorways, the M1 and the M62. It is in the form of a loop, which runs north from junction 27 of the M62 at Gildersome to the south of Leeds city centre and then south again to join up with the M1 at junction 43, near Rothwell. It is in this form because the M621 motorway was built in two separate parts. The western section from the M62 to Leeds was opened first in the years 1971–73 and was known as the 'South West Urban Motorway'. It terminated at a roundabout at what is now junction 3 of the M621. The northern end of the original route of the M1 terminated at junction 44 to the south-east of Leeds. However, in 1972 an extension off the M1 was built towards Leeds city centre and was called the 'South Eastern Motorway'. The two motorways should have been linked here, joining up with the North East Urban Motorway, which was never built. Instead, in 1999 the M1 was extended to join up with the A1 (M) at junction 48. The now defunct part of the M1 was renumbered the M621 and the two parts were joined up at a new junction 3 to form the current version of the M621. It is 7.7 miles (12.4 km) long.

The M621 coming into Leeds. Note the extension to the M1 going off on the right. (Wendy Chatterton)

M876

The M876 is an 8-mile-long (13 km) motorway in Scotland that connects the M80, near Denny, to the A876, near Kincardine Bridge. It helps to move traffic from the Glasgow area to Fife via the Kincardine and Clackmannanshire bridges over the River Firth. The motorway was opened in stages between 1965 and 1980.

There are two unusual features of this motorway. The first is that it shares its roadway with the M9 between junctions 2 and 3 for approximately a mile. It then continues as the M876 while the M9 goes off to the east. The M876 then ends as it becomes the A876, where the road splits just before crossing the River Forth into two routes – the A876 over the Clackmannanshire Bridge, and the A895 goes over the Kincardine Bridge. The second unusual feature is that there is a pedestrian foot crossing over part of the motorway. This is not on the actual main carriageway, but near the end of the Glenburvie Spur, a slip road for junction 2, near the junction with the A9 for Larbert. It is just before the end of motorway signs, so may have been an oversight by a civil servant somewhere.

One of just three examples on Britain's motorway network where two different motorways share the same piece of roadway. Here the M876 and the M9 run concurrent shortly before they divide at junction 7, looking eastbound. (Wendy Chatterton)

M898

The M898 in Renfrewshire is Scotland's shortest motorway at just half a mile (0.8 km) in length. It runs as a spur from junction 30 of the M8 to the Toll Plaza Interchange (junction 1), just before the Erskine Bridge on the A898. The bridge is the furthest west crossing of the River Clyde and until 2006 was a toll bridge – hence the name of the interchange. Locals call it the 'Spectacles Interchange' due to its similarity to a pair of spectacles when viewed from above. It carries traffic for Loch Lomond and the West Highlands, coming from the south of Scotland, wishing to avoid the A82 through Glasgow.

The M898 is Britain's highest numbered motorway and it first opened to motorists in December 1970. For five years, junction 1 of the M898 was the terminus of the M8, until it was extended further to its present end at junction 31.

Britain's highest numbered motorway joins the M8 with the Erskine Bridge to the west of Glasgow. (Wendy Chatterton)

3

A Roads that are Designated Motorways

A1 (M)

The A1, or Great North Road, as it is also known, is the most important A road in Britain, linking London with Edinburgh. It is 410 miles (660 km) long and is a mixture of single or dual carriageway and motorway. There are four separate sections of the A1 that are now designated motorway, which are discussed below. In total, there are approximately 150 miles (241 km) of motorway that make up these four sections. These were opened at different times between the years of 1961 and 2018.

Moving in a northerly direction from the southern end of the A1, the first section of A1 (M) motorway is approximately 24 miles (38 km) long and is between junction 1 (the M25) and junction 10 (Baldock). The first part of this section to be upgraded to motorway was the Stevenage Bypass (junctions 6 to 8) in May 1962. This was followed by the Baldock Bypass (junctions 8 to 10) in July 1967 and other sections until the final piece in this section between junctions 2 and 4 was opened in December 1986. This section includes the Hatfield Tunnel between junctions 3 and 4, which goes directly underneath the Galleria shopping centre.

The next section of motorway on the A1 is between junctions 14 and 17 (Alconbury to Peterborough), which was opened in 1998. The unusual thing about this section is that for most of its 13-mile (21 km) length there are four lanes on each carriageway.

The A1 (M), looking north towards the Hatfield Tunnel, which goes under the Galleria Shopping Centre. (Wendy Chatterton)

The A1 (M) in Hertfordshire, looking north towards junction 4 for the A414 to Hertford.

The third section, the Doncaster Bypass, between junctions 34 and 38, was the first section of the A1 to be opened as a motorway, as far back as July 1961. It was originally going to be part of the M1 through Yorkshire, but it lost out to the route past Sheffield and Leeds. It is one of the earliest sections of motorway in Britain and is due to be widened from two to three lanes in each direction. It is 15 miles (24 km) long.

The fourth and final section of the A1 (M) is the Darrington to Washington section, (junctions 40 to 65), which is the longest part of the A1 given over to motorway, at 93 miles (150 km) in length. It includes the junction where the M1 joins up with the A1 (M) at junction 43, and the well-known Scotch Corner Interchange at junction 53. The first part of this section to be opened was the Darlington Bypass (junctions 56 to 59) in May 1965, followed by the section east of Durham (junctions 59 to 63) in September 1969. The final piece of this stretch to open was that between junctions 51 and 56 (Leeming Bar to Barton) in March 2018, which was also the last piece of motorway to be opened in England at the time of writing. There is a possibility of this section being joined by upgraded motorway to the Doncaster section in the future, though no firm plans have been made at the time of writing.

The different sections of the A1 (M) on its route north pass the following towns and cities: Potters Bar, Hatfield, Welwyn Garden City, Stevenage, Letchworth, Peterborough, Doncaster, Pontefract, Castleford, Wetherby, Darlington, Durham, Chester-le-Street and Washington. It connects with the following motorways: M1, M18, M25, M62, A66 (M) and A194 (M). It is also part of Euroroute E15.

A3 (M)

The A3 (M) in Hampshire is the only motorway section on the A3 London to Portsmouth road. It links the A27 near Havant shortly before it becomes the M27, with the A3 north of Horndean. It is 5 miles (8.0 km) long and bypasses the towns of Waterlooville and Horndean, which was the reason it was built, as the original route of the A3 went through

Looking south down the A3 (M) in Hampshire towards the end of the motorway and the start of the A27.

these towns and couldn't be widened here. It joins the A27 2 miles before it becomes the M27, though it was originally planned as being continuous with the M27. The motorway passes through Portsdown Hill in a cutting that was the preferred option after the possibility of running the motorway through a tunnel here was dismissed.

A38 (M)

The A38 (M) is a 2-mile (3.2 km) section of the A38 in Birmingham that has been upgraded to motorway status. It starts at junction 6 of the M6, the Gravelly Hill Interchange, which is better known as 'Spaghetti Junction', before running south towards Birmingham city centre. The road itself is called the Aston Expressway, as it goes mainly through the Birmingham suburb of Aston. It was opened in May 1972 and its construction involved demolishing many houses to make way for the motorway. As it is an urban motorway used by a high number of vehicles each day there are frequent tailbacks. As such, it is called the 'Aston Distress Way' by locals.

It is unusual in that it does not have a central reservation keeping the two carriageways separate. Instead, it has a 'buffer lane' (coloured dark red) between the two flows of traffic. This usually makes up the middle of the seven lanes that are on most of this motorway. At off-peak times there are three lanes running in each direction, but in peak times a 'tidal flow' system is used where up to four lanes are used in the morning rush hour going into Birmingham, with just two coming out. Then in the evening rush hour this is reversed. There is also a 50-mph speed limit throughout.

The Aston Expressway A38 (M) in Birmingham, looking south towards the city centre. Note the missing central reservation

A48 (M)

The A48 (M) is a 2-mile-long (3.2 km) motorway spur running off the M4 at junction 29 into Cardiff and on to the A48 at junction 29A at St Mellons. When it first opened in 1977 this was the western end of the M4, but once the M4 was extended beyond Cardiff in 1980 it became the A48 (M). To confuse matters there was in fact a previous A48 (M) further to the west bypassing the town of Port Talbot in South Wales. It became the M4 when that was extended from the Cardiff area to Swansea.

The A48 (M), looking north, coming out of Cardiff shortly before it joins the M4. This spur was originally part of the M4. (David Watkins)

A57 (M)

The A57 (M), or the 'Mancunian Way' as it is better known, is a 2-mile-long (3.2 km) motorway going west to east just south of Manchester city centre. The majority of it is built on a flyover and it opened to traffic in March 1967 with a 30-mph speed limit. It was opened in May 1967 by the prime minister, Harold Wilson, as the A57 and was then upgraded to a motorway in the 1970s – hence the lack of hard shoulders. The speed limit was also raised to 50 mph.

One unusual feature is a slip road that suddenly stops 20 feet above the ground, though it is hidden by a large advertising board. It is the unfinished stub of a slip road that was supposed to go north into Manchester city centre, but this route never happened, even though the slip road had been partly built. The motorway also has no junctions along its route, apart from its start and finish.

The western end of the A57 (M), Mancunian Way in Manchester, looking west shortly before its elevated section. (Wendy Chatterton)

In August 2015, a large sink hole appeared at the eastern end of the motorway. The repairs took ten months to complete and cost £6 million to put right, due to a new sewer being built under the road.

At the eastern end of the Mancunian Way some people have argued that it changes into the A635 (M), as the A57 continues off the motorway to the south from the A6, while the motorway continues onto the A635. Although there are no street signs to show this, it is recorded as such in official Department for Transport documentation.

A58 (M)

The A58 (M) is part of the western section of the Leeds Inner Ring Road, which runs west to east to the north of Leeds city centre. This motorway starts at Wellington Street on the A58 west of Leeds city centre and goes as far as the North Street junction before continuing as the A64 (M) on the same stretch of motorway, so it is really one motorway

Looking south along the A58 (M) Leeds Inner Ring Road with the Westgate Tunnel in the background.

with two different numbers. It doesn't have any hard shoulders and runs in a deep cutting with several tunnels along its 1.5-mile (2.4 km) length. Prior to its opening in 1964 a lot of demolition of inner-city housing took place.

A64 (M)

The A64 (M) is part of the eastern section of the Leeds Inner Ring Road and was completed in 1969. It is a continuation of the A58 (M) in Leeds from the North Street junction to York Road where the A64 continues eastward and is dual carriageway throughout. It is approximately 0.5 mile (0.8 km) in length. The whole motorway was Britain's first ever urban motorway, opening before the Westway in London and the Mancunian Way in Manchester.

Looking east further along the same stretch of road in Leeds is the A64 (M). When this photo was taken in 2021 the Regent Street flyover was being rebuilt – hence the contraflow.

The A66 (M) in North Yorkshire looking northwards towards its terminus. (Wendy Chatterton)

A66 (M)

The A66 (M) is a short motorway spur from junction 57 of the A1 (M) that joins with the A66 continuing to Darlington and then Middlesbrough. It is known locally as the 'Blackwell Spur'. It was opened in 1965 at the same time as the A1 (M) in that area and is 2.2 miles (3.5 km) long. It is part of the route of the A66 from Penrith to Middlesbrough.

A74 (M)

This motorway is part of a single motorway route in Scotland that has two numbers – the M74 north of Abington in Scotland and the A74 (M) south of Abington. It runs from junction 13 of the motorway at Abington where the M74 ends, down to the Scottish border at Gretna (junction 22), where it continues onto the M6 in England, which in turn continues to Rugby where it meets the M1. The reason for this anomaly lies in its history. Originally the A74 was a single carriageway A road running from Carlisle in the south to Glasgow in the north. Over the years it was progressively altered to become a dual carriageway. However, the section in and around the south of Glasgow merited a new motorway, the M74, to be built to bypass these built-up areas. This was opened in 1969.

Looking north on the A74 (M) in southern Scotland. (Wendy Chatterton)

While the A74 was now a dual carriageway, there were calls to upgrade it to motorway standard with hard shoulders and grade separated junctions, so that there would eventually be a complete motorway between London and Glasgow. This did happen, and by 1999 the A74 had been upgraded to motorway standard. There have been several calls over the years for the motorway to be renumbered as the M74, or even the M6 to avoid confusion, but this has never materialised. The A74 (M) is notable for being the second highest motorway in Britain after the M62, where it reaches a height of over 1,000 feet above sea level near Beattock. It is 45 miles (72 km) long and also part of the Euroroute E05.

A167 (M)

This is an urban motorway that runs along the eastern edge of Newcastle city centre from the Tyne Bridge to Jesmond. The A167 (M) was originally known as the 'Central Motorway East', being the eastern part of three urban motorways that were planned to be built in Newcastle. In the end it was the only one that was built, due to rising costs and changes in political policy. It was opened in 1975 as the A1 (M) as this was the route of the A1 at the time and was then known as the 'Newcastle Central Motorway'. When the A1 (M) was moved further east to a route through the Tyne Tunnel the motorway number was changed to the A6127 (M). Finally, in 1990 it became the A167 (M) to fit in with the fact that Newcastle was now in the Motorway Zone 1 numbering system and not in Zone 6 anymore. It is just over 1 mile (1.8 km) in length.

The start of the A167 (M) in Newcastle-upon-Tyne, looking north. Note how it goes into a tunnel almost as soon as it starts.

The motorway has several notable features. As soon as it starts on the north side of Tyne Bridge it goes underground into a short tunnel under the Metro Radio building. Near its northern end it becomes a two-tier motorway, with the northbound lanes going directly over the southbound lanes on a flyover. Also, some of its exits go off to the right, as opposed to the left as is usual motorway practice.

A194 (M)

The A194 (M) is a short 4-mile (6.4 km) motorway that runs as a spur off the A1 (M) at junction 65 in Tyne and Wear and is part of the connecting trunk road from the A1 (M) to the A19 and the Tyne tunnels. The motorway has three junctions and was opened in 1970. It was renumbered as the A1 (M) when that route went east of Newcastle-Upon-Tyne via the Tyne Tunnel. However, in the 1980s when the A1 was rerouted to the west of Newcastle, this motorway once again became the A194 (M), making it the only motorway in Britain to lose its original number and then get it back again.

Looking north along the A194 (M) in Tyne and Wear, shortly before junction 2.

A308 (M)

The A308 (M) is a short motorway in Berkshire that runs as a spur off the M4 at junction 8/9 and is just 0.6 miles (0.97 km) long, making it one of the shortest motorways in Britain. At its northern end it joins up with the A308 at a roundabout that goes into Maidenhead town centre. It was opened in 1971 so that the A308 could still be connected with the M4 at the Holyport Interchange, junction 8/9. This new junction is so numbered as the original junction 8 was deemed to be too close to the new junction 8/9 and so was closed, meaning that the A308 needed a new junction with the M4. The A308 (M) was built to fill in this gap. Incidentally, junction 8/9 is the only double-numbered junction on the motorway network.

The A308 (M), near Maidenhead, shortly after its start, displaying 'end of motorway' signs. At just over half a mile in length, it is one of Britain's shortest motorways.

The A329 (M) in Berkshire, looking south to its junction with the M4. Note the very wide central reservation, which was created like this in case a third lane was ever added to each carriageway.

A329 (M)

This is a 4-mile (6.4 km) motorway that links the western edge of Bracknell to the south eastern edge of Reading. The motorway was constructed in the years 1972 to 1975 and originally went as far as the A4 east of Reading. In the 1990s the motorway west of Winnersh Triangle was downgraded to the A3290 when a Park and Ride bus service began that used the hard shoulder as its route. The A329 (M) goes over the M4 in a free-flow interchange, which was designed to be part of a future M31 that would have joined up with the M3. Part of this plan was to increase the dual carriageway on the motorway to three lanes each way and the wide grass-covered central reservation in the section north of the M4 is a leftover of this plan. The motorway is managed by Wokingham Borough Council.

A404 (M)

This is a 2.4-mile-long (3.9 km) motorway that links junction 8/9 of the M4 in the south to the A404 at junction 9B in the north, which in turn connects with junction 4 of the

Looking towards the end of the A404 (M) as it approaches the Holyport Interchange, junction 8/9 of the M4 – the only double-numbered motorway junction in the country.

M40 at High Wycombe. It is dual carriageway throughout and is known locally as the M4/M40 Link Road or the Maidenhead and Marlow Bypass. This is because when it was first opened in 1961 as the A4 (M) it was part of the Maidenhead Bypass, running from junction 7 of the M4 to the A4 west of Maidenhead. Two years later in 1963 it was renumbered M4 as part of the Slough Bypass, which was extended eastwards from junction 7 to junction 5 of the M4. The proposed route of the M4 westwards from here was to go north of Reading, but this was later changed to go to the south instead, so the M4 today goes south-west here from junction 8/9. This redundant section of the M4 was then renumbered the A423 (M) and finally the A404 (M) and joins to the M4 at the Holyport Interchange, junction 8/9.

A601 (M)

This motorway was the original route of the M6, being part of the Lancaster Bypass when it opened in 1960. However, when the M6 was rerouted towards the north and east in 1970 it became the A601 (M), in spite of the fact that there wasn't in fact an A601 road in the vicinity. (The actual A601 is in fact in Derby.) It runs for 1.3 miles (2.1 km) from junction 35 of the M6 to join up with the A6 to the north of Carnforth in Lancashire. It is dual carriageway with a hard shoulder and in 2021 it was announced that Lancashire County Council was applying for it to be downgraded from a motorway to save on costs.

The A601 (M) motorway near Carnforth in Lancashire, looking north. Note the hedge growing on the central reservation. (Michael Webster)

A627 (M)

This motorway links the towns of Rochdale and Oldham in Greater Manchester and goes over the M62 to the east of Manchester. It is 3.5 miles (5.6 km) long and was opened in 1972. It is unusual in that about halfway along it meets the M62 at junction 20, at a roundabout with traffic lights. There should really be a flyover here taking the A627 (M) over the M62, but this has never been built, so traffic has to leave the A627 (M) to get to the other part of it. The probable reason for this is that the northern section was built as a spur from the M62 into Rochdale, while the southern section was originally part of the A663, known as the 'Broadway Extension', taking traffic from Oldham to the M62. As they both met at junction 20 back in 1972, someone decided to change the two roads into one motorway – the A627 (M). Another unusual feature is that at the Oldham end there is a 1-mile (1.6km) spur, known as 'Slattocks Link', leading from the motorway, which some argue should be numbered the A6138 (M).

Looking towards the Thornham Interchange, which splits the A627 (M) into two distinct parts as it crosses over the M62 in Greater Manchester. (Wendy Chatterton)

The contentious A635 (M) at the eastern end of the Mancunian Way, believed to be the shortest section of motorway in Britain.

A635 (M)

The A635 (M) in Manchester is arguably the shortest motorway in Britain. It is found at the eastern end of the Mancunian Way, which is numbered the A57 (M) on road signs and maps. People argue that the section from where the flyover goes over the A6 to its end on the A635 is actually the A635 (M) as it links onto the A635, rather than the A57. While the A635 (M) isn't actually signposted as such on this section of the motorway, it was referred to as a motorway in the Department for Transport document entitled 'Statutory Instrument 1995 No. 3266'. This section of the Mancunian Way is just 0.3 miles in length.

A823 (M)

This is a short motorway spur of 1 mile (1.6 km) off the M90 on the north side of the Queensferry Crossing in Fife, Scotland. It leads onto the A823 towards Dunfermline. The reason it exists is that it was meant to be a part of a much longer motorway, the M92, which was envisaged as running from the Kincardine Bridge in the west to Glenrothes in the east. It was opened in 1964 along with the part of the M90, to which it connects and provides a quick link to the M90 for traffic from Dunfermline.

The start of the A823 (M) where it leaves junction 2 of the M90 in Fife, Scotland, soon after the Queensferry Crossing. (Wendy Chatterton)

4

Former Motorways

The following are former motorways that have been downgraded to A or B roads.

M10: Opened from the M1 to St Albans (A1/A6) in 1959. It became part of the A414 in 2009.

M41: A spur road from Shepherd's Bush to the A40 (M). It became the A3220 in 2000.

A8 (M): A short spur from the M73 and M80 to the A8, which became part of the A8 in 2017.

The former M41, which linked parts of West London with the A40 (M) Westway. It is now the A3220.

The famous 'Westway' flyover in West London, which used to be the A40 (M), but has been the A40 since 2000 when Transport for London took over this road.

A18 (M): A spur from the M18, most of which is now the M180.

A40 (M): Built between 1962 and 1970, this is the Westway Flyover in West London, which became the A40 in 2000.

A41 (M): The Tring Bypass, which opened in 1973. Now part of the A41 Watford/M25 to Aylesbury trunk road.

A46 (M): Part of a spur from the M1 to Leicester city centre. Now part of the A5460.

A102 (M): This was a motorway running either side of the Blackwall Tunnel in East London. In 2000 the northern section became part of the A12 and the southern section became part of the A102.

A329 (M): In the 1990s the northern section of the A329 (M) from Winnersh Triangle to the A4 was downgraded to the A329 so it could be used by Park & Ride buses.

A601 (M): This refers to the southern section of the A601 (M), which was downgraded to become the B6601 in 2020.

A666 (M): This motorway near Bolton opened in December 1971. It is now a spur off the M61 and leads to the A666 and Bolton.

A6144 (M): Originally ran from the M60 at junction 8 to the A6144. It existed from 1987 to 2006 when it was downgraded to the A6144.

The southern section of the former A601 (M), which was a motorway from 1987 until 2020 and was Britain's narrowest motorway. (Wendy Chatterton)

5

Other Motorways

M96

This is found at the Fire Service College in Moreton-on-the-Marsh in Gloucestershire. It is built on a former RAF base where part of the runway has been turned into a motorway called the 'M96', which is used as a training space for the emergency services.

M101

An imaginary motorway used in the book *Blott on the Landscape* by Tom Sharpe.

M104

The number of the motorway in the 1968 Thunderbirds film, *Thunderbird Six*, which shows a Tiger Moth biplane flying under a bridge on the yet to be opened M40.

M399

Another imaginary motorway that was used in the BBC TV series *Blott on the Landscape*, which was based on the book of the same name.

A sign showing the M96 at the Fire Service College in Gloucestershire. (Fire Service College)

Other Information

Websites

Motorwayservices.uk
Patheticmotorways.co.uk
Roads.org.uk
Sabre-roads.org.uk

Further Reading

Charlesworth, George, *A History of Britain's Motorways*
Chatterton, Mark, *British Motorways: An Introduction*
Jackson, Mike *M6 Sights Guide*
Jackson, Mike and Kristina Thimm, *M5 Sights Guide*
Phippen, Roy, *M25 Travelling Clockwise*

Acknowledgements

I would like to thank the following people and websites for their help in providing information and photographs for use in this book: Carole Jeffcock and Kay Chaonsri at the Fire Service College, Moreton-in-Marsh; Paul Sellars at Lancashire County Council; Suiad Hussain at National Highways; David Boreham at North Lincolnshire Council; John Randall at Motorway Services Online; Pathetic Motorways; Roads.org.uk and Sabre-roads. org.uk.

Thank you to Nilfanion and Dr Greg (© OpenStreetMap contributors. Contains Ordnance Survey data © Crown copyright and database right 2010) for the source material for both maps used in this book.

Thanks also to the following people for providing their own photographs for use in this book: Allan Heron, Howard Johnston, Andrew Lamyman, Peter McDermott, Carol Park, Ian Park, David Watkins, John Webb and Michael Webster. Plus the taxi drivers of Bradford, Leeds, Maidenhead and Portsmouth who drove me to visit the motorways in their towns and cities. Last, but not least, a big thank you to my wife, Wendy, who has been with me all the way on this journey and who took many of the photographs for this book.

All photographs by the author unless otherwise stated.